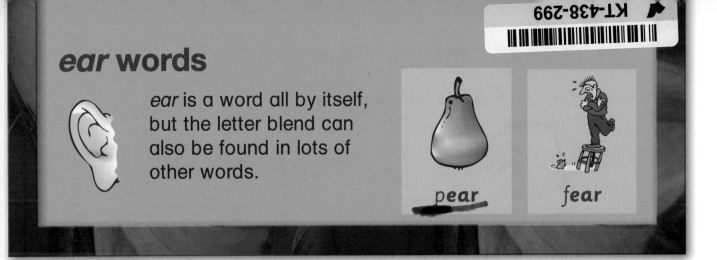

ear words

ear is a word all by itself, but the letter blend can also be found in lots of other words.

pear

fear

I Draw a pearl shape round all the *ear* words. Then write them in the spaces below.

hear	tearing	bare	tear	fear	fair	wear
smear	bear	bowl	pearl	heard	herd	

a _____

b _____

c _____

d _____

e _____

f _____

g _____

h _____

i _____

II Help the bear collect the honey pots with *ear* words inside. Colour them in, then write the words below.

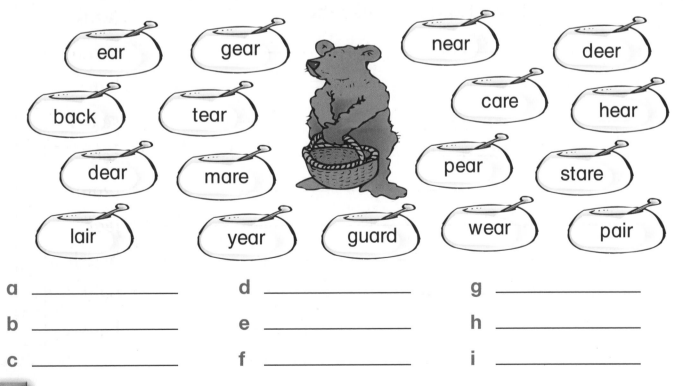

a _____

b _____

c _____

d _____

e _____

f _____

g _____

h _____

i _____

8

ea words

We find the *ea* blend in lots of words.

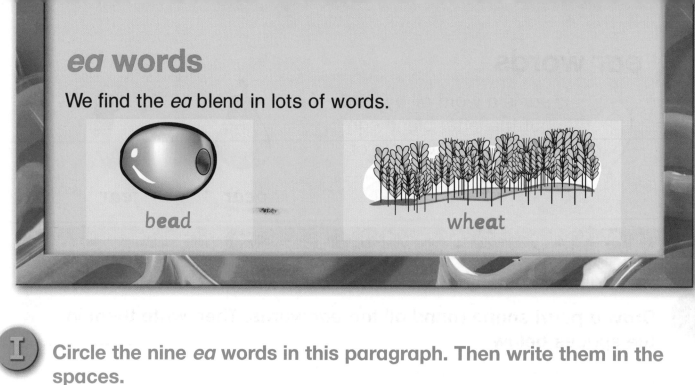

bead   wheat

I Circle the nine *ea* words in this paragraph. Then write them in the spaces.

I sat on the seat to eat my tea. I looked at the sea as I ate my pie and peas, followed by peaches and cream. Then I washed my sticky face clean and started to read.

a _____   d _____   g _____

b _____   e _____   h _____

c _____   f _____   i _____

II Write a story that uses all of these *ea* words and tick them off the list as you use them.

_____

_____

_____

_____

_____

_____

_____

_____

_____

_____

weak ☐

mean ☐

leaf ☐

search ☐

sea ☐

team ☐

fear ☐

beach ☐

beat ☐

beak ☐

wh blends

Lots of words use the sound **wh**oo!

Lots of question words start with the blend *wh*.

I This little ghost is making the sound whoo! He has found a set of cards with *wh* words on. Colour in the card in each set that contains the blend *wh*.

a wheel | wink | water

b wait | white | wellington

c whale | wall | watch

d will | whisk | weight

e wham | winkle | witch

f win | whimper | wand

g wind | swim | whisper

h wag | while | west

II Make up questions, using each of these words that begin with *wh*.

| what | who | where | when | which | why |

a _____

b _____

c _____

d _____

e _____

f _____

ch blends

Do you prefer **ch**ips or **ch**ocolate? They are both tasty and they both start with the letter blend *ch*.

II The words under these boxes all use the *ch* blend. Draw a picture of these things.

a [ ]

chick

c [ ]

lunch

e [ ]

chin

b [ ]

chimp

d [ ]

child

f [ ]

chip

I Underline the *ch* blends in each word. Then write a sentence using that word.

a chill _____

b much _____

c chest _____

d rich _____

e check _____

f such _____

g bench _____

h bunch _____

Breaking words down

When you spell words, it is useful to break them into smaller chunks. This helps when you are reading, too.

Drawing could be easily broken into dr-aw-ing.

I **Break these words into small chunks. Then learn to spell them.**

a **snail**   breaks down into   _____-_____

b **writing**   breaks down into   _____-_____

c **hotel**   breaks down into   _____-_____

d **maybe**   breaks down into   _____-_____

e **donkey**   breaks down into   _____-_____

f **flowers**   breaks down into   _____-_____

g **carrot**   breaks down into   _____-_____

h **important**   breaks down into   _____-_____-_____

i **computer**   breaks down into   _____-_____-_____

II **Write the missing chunks of each word. Use the words in the box to help you.**

| because |
| brother |
| sister |
| would |
| jump |
| should |
| jumping |
| another |

a sh-_____-ld

b br-_____-er

c be-cau-_____

d w-_____-_____

e j-_____-_____

f _____-um-_____

g sis-_____

h an-_____-_____

12

Verbs

Verbs are the action words in a sentence. They tell you what is being done. Some people call them '**doing words**'.

Lick is a **verb**. It tells us what is being done.

I **Underline the verbs in each sentence.**

a The bird flew away.

b The girl laughed at her brothers.

c The mother ate a big slice of cake.

d The snake slid across the rocks.

e The lion roared.

f The two brothers were shouting very loudly!

g The mouse squeaked as it ran.

h The sun shone brightly.

i I ran down the street.

II **Complete each sentence with a verb that makes sense. Use the words in the box to help you.**

a The giraffe _____ leaves from high branches.

b The dog _____ at the postman.

c My dad _____ very loudly!

d The teacher _____ her name on the board.

e The spider _____ in the corner.

f The horse _____ away.

g The cat _____ because it was happy.

h The waves _____ up the beach.

Verbs

snores
purred
roared
ate
wrote
galloped
barked
lurked

Tenses

The words we write tell us whether things are happening now, in the past or in the future.

I am walking is the **present** – now.

I walked   is in the **past**.

I shall walk   is in the **future**.

Write down whether these sentences are in the past, present or future tense.

a I sat on the chair. _____

b I went to the party. _____

c I'll see you in the morning. _____

d She saw a cat. _____

e I shall go to school tomorrow. _____

f I am laughing. _____

g I can see a rainbow! _____

h I ran all the way home. _____

i I am reading a great story. _____

j I am swimming. _____

Cross out the wrong verb tense in each sentence.

a I **wented went** to school today.

b I **seen saw** a whale!

c Did you **see saw** that sunset?

d Who **ran runned** the fastest?

e I **won winned** the race!

f I **catched caught** the ball.

g He **seed saw** the film today.

h I **goed went** to my Granny's yesterday.

i I **caught catched** a cold.

j Who **wented went** to the park this morning?

14

Vowels and consonants

Vowels are the letters **a e i o u**

Consonants are the other letters in the alphabet:
b c d f g h j k l m n p q r s t v w x y z

Most English words contain at least one vowel:
Man sit cake

Y is a strange letter, because it can act like a vowel.

Y acts like a vowel in some words: **Fly cry my**

I Fill in the vowels to complete these words.

a c __ ll __ d

b l __ k __

c sh __ __ ld

d b __ c __ __ se

e m __ y b __

f s __ st __ r

g br __ th __ r

h w __ __ ld

i w h __ t

j c __ __ ld

II Make as many three letter words as you can by putting different vowels in the spaces. The first one has been started for you.

a c __ t   <u>cat</u>

b p __ n   _____

c b __ n   _____

d d __ g   _____

e b __ g   _____

f h __ t   _____

g d __ d   _____

h p __ t   _____

i b __ d   _____

j l __ p   _____

Compound words

Compound words are made from smaller words joined together, without changing the spelling.

butter + fly = butterfly

Ⅰ Draw a line to match the parts of the compound words to make new words.

a news   lid

b sand   castle

c flower   bird

d lady   pot

e eye   paper

f hand   case

g bed   bag

h stair   room

i note   up

j make   book

Ⅱ Use the words in the box to make 10 compound words.

| all | crow | fish | board | stick | day | bull | skate | stack | week |

a scare _____

b _____ board

c star _____

d cup _____

e hay _____

f birth _____

g _____ dog

h lip _____

i _____ end

j over _____

Syllables

Syllables are the **chunks of sound** that make up words. If you say words out loud, you can hear the syllables.

bathroom has two syllables:
bath + room

crocodile has three syllables:
croc + o + dile

I **Count the syllables in each word. Then write the answer in the box.**

a caterpillar ☐

b leaf ☐

c garden ☐

d rainbow ☐

e spider ☐

f butterfly ☐

g ladybird ☐

h bird ☐

i hedgehog ☐

j greenhouse ☐

II **Rewrite the words in order, with the words with the lowest number of syllables first.**

a daisy rose buttercup _____ _____ _____

b chinchilla cat rabbit _____ _____ _____

c planet sun universe _____ _____ _____

d sausages eggs bacon _____ _____ _____

e orange banana lime _____ _____ _____

f pen pencil computer _____ _____ _____

g telephone mobile talk _____ _____ _____

h tea chocolate coffee _____ _____ _____

i sandwiches cake trifle _____ _____ _____

j scorpion ant beetle _____ _____ _____

Synonyms

Synonyms are words that mean the same, or nearly the same, thing.

Sad and *unhappy* are synonyms.

I Match the synonyms with a line.

a insects   flame

b larger   toss

c near   bugs

d small   fastest

e shining   bigger

f throw   close

g shout   tiny

h quickest   sparkling

i fire   yell

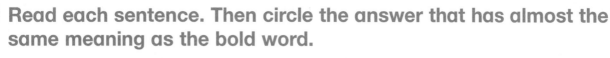

II Read each sentence. Then circle the answer that has almost the same meaning as the bold word.

a That is a **huge** dog!   enormous   small   scary

b The boy **pushed** the bike out of the way.   raced   shoved   changed

c I **like** sweets.   eat   enjoy   hate

d The girls **laughed** at the joke.   smiled   frowned   giggled

e The lion **ran** quickly.   sprinted   skipped   walked

f The man **drank** his lemonade.   spilled   tipped   swigged

g The lady **sobbed** because she was sad.   cried   frowned   sighed

h The stars **shone** in the sky.   hung   stood   twinkled

Homophones

Homophones are words that sound the same even if they have a different meaning or spelling. Homophones may also be spelled the same, such as bear (animal) and bear (carry or put up with).

An example would be:

two the number 2
too as well
to as in *going to*

I Draw a line to match the homophones.

a isle   pear

b allowed   beach

c ate   deer

d I   bare

e bear   I'll

f beech   eye

g pair   eight

h creek   creak

i dear   aloud

II Cross out the homophone in each sentence that does not make sense.

a My auntie said I had **grown groan** since she last saw me.

b My **hare hair** is blonde.

c Can I come **two too**?

d A **herd heard** of sheep ran towards me.

e The **hole whole** class said hello.

f **Our Hour** cat likes fish.

g I **know no** your name.

h I **moan mown** if I have toothache.

19

Suffix *ly*

In this sentence, the word **carefully** is an adverb. It tells how the girl made the model. The *ly* at the end is a **suffix**, added to the word **careful**. By adding *ly* we make an adverb that tells us how something happens or is done.

*The girl made the model plane **carefully**.*

 Complete each sentence with the correct adverb from the box.

| happily   kindly   lazily   delicately   roughly   selfishly   sadly |

a The swimmer rubbed herself _____ with the towel.

b The boy _____ shared his sweets.

c The cat stretched out _____ on the chair.

d My grandma smiled _____ when she saw me coming.

e The man frowned _____.

f The butterfly fluttered _____ from flower to flower.

g The boy _____ said he would not share his toys.

 Match the adverb to the correct description.

a carefully   shining

b bravely   fast

c brightly   done with care

d beautifully   not afraid

e perfectly   not done well

f quickly   moving in a delicate way

g badly   done in a lovely way

h gracefully   absolutely correct

Suffix *ful*

The letters *ful* can be added to the end of words as a *suffix*. When you add the suffix *ful* to a word, you are saying that it is **full of** something.

A spoon**ful** of sugar is a spoon **full of** sugar.

 I **Write the new word, using the suffix *ful*, in the space.**

a Full of hope [hope + ful] = _____

b Full of joy [joy + ful] = _____

c Full of peace [peace + ful] = _____

d Full of sorrow [sorrow + ful] = _____

e Full of colour [colour + ful] = _____

f Full of doubt [doubt + ful] = _____

g Full of cheer [cheer + ful] = _____

h Full of power [power + ful] = _____

i Full of thought [thought + ful] = _____

 II **Write out the meaning of each word.**

a wonderful _____

b playful _____

c useful _____

d helpful _____

e hopeful _____

f joyful _____

g truthful _____

h beautiful _____

i hateful _____

21

Using an index

An index is found in some **non-fiction** books. It helps readers to find information they need. It is in alphabetical order so it is easy to find things.

Look at this index. Write down which page numbers you need to look at to find out more.

| Apples 67, 71 |
| Cats 16, 18, 90 |
| Frost 24, 43 |
| Nests 15 |

a To read about apples, I would find pages [   ].

b To read about cats, I would find pages [   ].

c To read about nests, I would find page [   ].

d To read about frost, I would find pages [   ].

This index has been mixed up. Rewrite it in the correct order. Remember, it should be alphabetical.

| goldfish 26 |
| snail 31 |
| water 76 |
| shrew 31, 66 |
| gnat 22 |
| moth 54 |
| iris 12 |
| bat 1, 14 |
| worm 42, 59 |
| willow 37 |

a _____

b _____

c _____

d _____

e _____

f _____

g _____

h _____

i _____

j _____

Tricky spellings

Some words do not seem to follow spelling rules or are difficult to work out by saying out loud. You just have to learn them by heart.

| every | gnat | neither |

I Here are some tricky words. Write them out, then try to learn them. Use look, cover, write, check to learn.

a only _____   f could _____

b little _____   g would _____

c down _____   h should _____

d their _____   i does _____

e because _____   j goes _____

II Spend a few minutes looking at each word. Cover it up. Then try to write it from memory. Check your spelling against the original.

a mother _____

b father _____

c always _____

d once _____

e upon _____

f after _____

g every _____

h eight _____

i brother _____

j before _____

Time words

Words can be used to show when something happens.

next   after   before   during

I Complete each sentence using a word from the box. You may use the words more than once.

a Snow had fallen _____ the night.

b I brush my teeth _____ I go to bed.

c _____ school, I have a swimming lesson.

d _____ dinner, I often have some ice cream.

e I have eaten a lolly and _____ I would like a bag of crisps.

f _____ we went to the cinema, we went shopping because we had seen an advertisement for cheap videos before the film.

g We had our dinner _____ we went out so we would not be hungry.

h _____ I was born, my mum and dad lived in the town.

> *next   after*
> *before   during*

II Now write two sentences using each time word below.

before a _____

b _____

after c _____

d _____

during e _____

f _____

next g _____

h _____

firstly i _____

j _____

Writing stories

Do you like writing stories? There are things you need to remember if you want to make your stories exciting:

- an exciting beginning to tempt the reader to continue

- descriptions of where the story happens

- interesting descriptions of characters

- exciting dialogue – what the characters say.

I **You are going to write a story. First, imagine what your characters are like and make them seem real!**

a What do they look like? _____

b What are their clothes like? _____

c What are their voices like? _____

d How do they walk? _____

e Do they have a favourite food? _____

f How do they act with their friends? _____

g Do they have a problem to solve, or a challenge to face?

_____

II **Now make notes about where your story is set. Use your senses and imagine you are there. Then write your story!**

a Where is your story set? _____

b What can you see? _____

c Can you smell anything? _____

d Describe how things feel – like rough tree bark or a cold window.

_____

e Can you hear anything? _____

f Can you taste anything – like a salty sea breeze? _____

Commas in a list

When you make a list of things in a sentence, you should separate them with commas and put the word 'and' between the last two things on the list.

I bought some eggs, potatoes, carrots, bananas and peppers.

I **Add commas in the correct place for each sentence.**

a I like cats dogs and rabbits.

b I read books comics and newspapers.

c My favourite foods are cake toast and oranges.

d I collected shells stones and seaweed to decorate my sandcastle.

e Rainbows are red orange yellow green blue indigo and violet.

f It is cold so put on a hat scarf and gloves.

g I drink orange juice cola and milk.

h I saw tigers lions and hippos at the zoo.

II **Make up sentences of your own about these things. Include lists and don't forget the commas.**

a animals _____

b games _____

c clothes _____

d toys _____

e vegetables _____

f plants _____

g bugs _____

h sports _____

Questions

Question marks show when a question has been asked.

Are we there yet?

Special question words also give us clues that questions are being asked:

Why   Where

When   What

Who   Which   How

I **Add the question marks to these sentences.**

a   What is your name

b   'Can I come too ' asked Mary.

c   Why can't I That's not fair!

d   Would you like a sweet

e   Why not I want to!

f   Do you like snakes

g   Do you want to come with me I don't mind.

h   Can we go today

i   Who was that

j   Would anyone like some supper

II **Choose a word from the box to make each sentence make sense. You can use the words more than once.**

why	where	when	what	who

a   _____ said that?

b   _____ are my keys?

c   _____ is your name?

d   _____ did you do that?

e   _____ time is it?

f   _____ is my pen?

g   _____ can we go to the park?

h   _____ would like to play with me

i   _____ shall we go shopping?

j   _____ would you like to drink?

Writing *ai, ar, un*

It is important to practise your handwriting, so that people can read all the good things you write about!

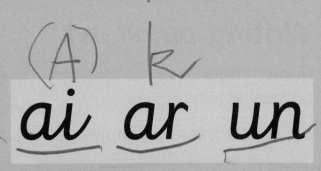

ai ar un

I

Copy these words to practise joining *a* and *i*.

a airy _airy_

b brain _brain_

c drain _drain_

d fairy _fairy_

e air _air_

f train _train_

g fair _fair_

h chair _chair_

i dairy _dairy_

j chain _chain_

II

Now copy these *ar* and *un* words.

a shark _shark_

b dark _dark_

c bark _bark_

d car _car_

e bar _bar_

f bun _bun_

g fun _fun_

h under _under_

Writing *ou, vi, wi*

Some letters have
horizontal joins.

ou, vi and *wi* are examples.

ou vi wi

I Copy the *ou* words.

a **you** _____

b **could** _____

c **would** _____

d **should** _____

e **mouth** _____

f **youth** _____

g **bought** _____

h **fought** _____

i **drought** _____

j **found** _____

II Now copy the *vi* and *wi* words.

a **vitamin** _____

b **vine** _____

c **wink** _____

d **win** _____

e **wind** _____

f **visit** _____

g **video** _____

h **wife** _____

Writing *ab, ul, it*

Some handwriting patterns are difficult, because they join a small letter to a tall letter.

ab ul it

I Now copy the words.

a about _____

b baby _____

c table _____

d able _____

e cable _____

f dab _____

g rabbit _____

h habit _____

i label _____

j tabby _____

II Now copy these *ul* and *it* words.

a full _____

b bit _____

c bite _____

d hit _____

e bull _____

f kite _____

g lit _____

h pull _____

Writing *ol, wh, ot*

These handwriting joins are quite tricky, but the more you practise, the easier it will become.

ol   wh   ot

I Copy these words in your best handwriting.

a hot *hot*

b why *why*

c when *when*

d which *which*

e who *who*

f otter *otter*

g other *other*

h got *got*

i dot *dots*

j what *what*

II Now copy these words.

a doll *doll*

b hold *hold*

c fold *fold*

d mole *mole*

e sold *sold*

f told *told*

g golly *golly*

h lolly

ANSWERS

Page 2

I
- **a** bars, park
- **b** far
- **c** hard, dark
- **d** card, Mark
- **e** jar, garden
- **f** barn, car
- **g** warm
- **h** hard
- **i** postcard

II
- **a** park
- **b** mark
- **c** bark
- **d** sparks
- **e** car
- **f** far
- **g** dark
- **h** farm
- **i** tarmac

Page 3

I Words learned with correct spellings.

II Any sentences containing the words. Samples shown below.
- **a** The boy played in the park.
- **b** My teddy is my favourite toy.
- **c** I jumped for joy when I scored a goal.
- **d** The dog will destroy my homework if she gets hold of it!
- **e** I enjoy cake.
- **f** Flies annoy me.
- **g** A queen is royal.
- **h** I enjoyed your party!
- **i** I am enjoying this film.

Page 4

I
- **a** A black bird.
- **b** To cut grass.
- **c** Something to eat soup from.
- **d** White, cold flakes that fall from the sky.
- **e** A pointed, wooden stick that is fired from a bow.
- **f** Where your arm is able to bend.
- **g** The day after today.
- **h** To get bigger.

II Circled: yellow, pillow, row, slowest, follow, show, marrow, own.
Any sentences containing the words which show the child understands the meaning of each word.

Page 5

I
- **a** paired
- **b** hair
- **c** airy
- **d** hairy
- **e** stair
- **f** fair
- **g** lair
- **h** pair
- **i** fairy
- **j** fairest

II
- **a** who is the fairest of them all?
- **b** at the top of the Christmas tree.
- **c** when I went to the fair.
- **d** so that makes a pair!
- **e** because it has large windows that open.
- **f** into the dragon's lair.
- **g** to go to bed.
- **h** a big hairy spider.
- **i** to make myself neat and tidy.
- **j** my teacher paired me up with my best friend.

Page 6

I Pictures of:
- **a** cork
- **b** torch
- **c** cord
- **d** horse
- **e** storm
- **f** fork

II Coloured in: form, afford, north, snort, scorch, porch, worn, sport, morning, port

Page 7

I Pictures matched to correct word.

II Any sentences that make sense and contain the *er* words. Examples given below:
- **a** My tea is hotter than I can bear!
- **b** My cat is fatter than my dog.
- **c** My sister is smaller than her friends.
- **d** My nails are sharper than needles!
- **e** My house is bigger than yours.
- **f** This river is wider than the River Tyne.
- **g** It feels much colder today.
- **h** This sock is smellier than mine!
- **i** You are sillier than my brother!

Page 8

I hear, smear, tearing, bear, tear, pearl, fear, heard, wear

II Coloured in: ear, dear, gear, tear, year, near, pear, wear, hear

Page 9

I
- **a** seat
- **b** eat
- **c** tea
- **d** sea
- **e** peas
- **f** peaches
- **g** cream
- **h** clean
- **i** read

II A story containing all of the *ea* words in the box.

Page 10

I
- **a** wheel
- **b** white
- **c** whale
- **d** whisk
- **e** wham
- **f** whimper
- **g** whisper
- **h** while

II Any questions using what, who, where, when, which, why.
For example: What is the time? Who is that? Where are we? When will we go out? Which cake is mine? Why are you late?

Page 11

I Pictures of:
- **a** chick
- **b** chimp
- **c** lunch
- **d** child
- **e** chin
- **f** chip

II Any sentences that make sense and contain the given words.
- **a** <u>ch</u>ill
- **b** mu<u>ch</u>
- **c** <u>ch</u>est
- **d** ri<u>ch</u>
- **e** <u>ch</u>eck
- **f** su<u>ch</u>
- **g** ben<u>ch</u>
- **h** bun<u>ch</u>

Page 12

I There is no right way to segment these words; your child should break them down in any way that makes them easy to remember. Here are some suggestions:
- **a** sn - ail
- **b** writ - ing
- **c** ho - tel
- **d** may - be
- **e** don - key
- **f** flow - ers
- **g** car - rot
- **h** imp - ort - ant
- **i** com - put - er

II
- **a** ou
- **b** oth
- **c** se
- **d** ou - ld
- **e** ump - ing
- **f** j - p
- **g** ter
- **h** oth - er

Page 13

I
- **a** flew
- **b** laughed
- **c** ate
- **d** slid
- **e** roared
- **f** shouting
- **g** squeaked
- **h** shone
- **i** ran

II
- **a** ate
- **b** barked
- **c** snores
- **d** wrote
- **e** lurked
- **f** galloped
- **g** purred
- **h** roared

Page 14

I
- **a** past
- **b** past
- **c** future
- **d** past
- **e** future
- **f** present
- **g** present
- **h** past
- **i** present
- **j** present

II Cross out:
- **a** wented
- **b** seen
- **c** saw
- **d** runned
- **e** winned
- **f** catched
- **g** seed
- **h** goed
- **i** catched
- **j** wented

Page 15

I
- **a** called
- **b** like
- **c** should
- **d** because
- **e** maybe
- **f** sister
- **g** brother
- **h** would
- **i** what
- **j** could

II
- **a** cat, cut, cot
- **b** pan, pen, pin, pun
- **c** ban, Ben, bin, bun
- **d** dig, dog, dug
- **e** bag, beg, big, bog, bug
- **f** hat, hit, hot, hut
- **g** dad, did, dud
- **h** pat, pet, pit, pot, put
- **i** bad, bed, bid, bud
- **j** lap, lip, lop

Page 16

I
a paper
b castle
c pot
d bird
e lid
f bag
g room
h case
i book
j up

II
a scarecrow
b skateboard
c starfish
d cupboard
e haystack
f birthday
g bulldog
h lipstick
i weekend
j overall

Page 17

I
a 4
b 1
c 2
d 2
e 2
f 3
g 3
h 1
i 2
j 2

II
a rose daisy buttercup
b cat rabbit chinchilla
c sun planet universe
d eggs bacon sausages
e lime orange banana
f pen pencil computer
g talk mobile telephone
h tea coffee chocolate
i cake trifle sandwiches
j ant beetle scorpion

Page 18

I
a bugs
b bigger
c close
d tiny
e sparkling
f toss
g yell
h fastest
i flame

II
a enormous
b shoved
c enjoy
d giggled
e sprinted
f swigged
g cried
h twinkled

Page 19

I
a I'll
b aloud
c eight
d eye
e bare
f beach
g pear
h creak
i deer

II Cross out:
a groan
b hare
c two
d heard
e hole
f Hour
g no
h mown

Page 20

I
a roughly
b kindly
c lazily
d happily
e sadly
f delicately
g selfishly

II
a done with care
b not afraid
c shining
d done in a lovely way
e absolutely correct
f fast
g not done well
h moving in a delicate way

Page 21

I
a hopeful
b joyful
c peaceful
d sorrowful
e colourful
f doubtful
g cheerful
h powerful
i thoughtful

II Any correct answers. Some suggestions are given below:
a fabulous; a really good thing.
b messing about in a happy way; playing games.
c something that can be used to carry out jobs; just what is needed.
d someone who is willing to help and make themselves useful.
e full of hope (perhaps that something will or will not happen).
f very happy.
g does not lie; tells the truth.
h lovely; attractive.
i horrid; nasty.

Page 22

I
a apples pages 67 and 71
b cats pages 16, 18 and 90
c nests page 15
d frost pages 24 and 43

II
a bat 1, 14
b gnat 22
c goldfish 26
d iris 12
e moth 54
f shrew 31, 66
g snail 31
h water 76
i willow 37
j worm 42, 59

Page 23

I Words learned and spelt correctly.

II Words learned and spelt correctly.

Page 24

I
a during
b before
c After
d After
e next
f After
g before
h Before

II Any sentences correctly using the 'time' words such as 'I have a bath before I go to bed'.

Page 25

I Any suitable answers describing a character's voice, clothing, appearance etc.

II Any suitable answers exploring the setting of the story – the more descriptive the better!

Page 26

I
a I like cats, dogs and rabbits.
b I read books, comics and newspapers.
c My favourite foods are cake, toast and oranges.
d I collected shells, stones and seaweed to decorate my sandcastle.
e Rainbows are red, orange, yellow, green, blue, indigo and violet.
f It is cold so put on a hat, scarf and gloves.
g I drink orange juice, cola and milk.
h I saw tigers, lions and hippos at the zoo.

II Any sensible sentences including lists (with commas) about the subjects given.

Page 27

I
a What is your name?
b 'Can I come too?' asked Mary.
c Why can't I? That's not fair!
d Would you like a sweet?
e Why not? I want to!
f Do you like snakes?
g Do you want to come with me? I don't mind.
h Can we go today?
i Who was that?
j Would anyone like some supper?

II
a Who
b Where
c What
d Why of When
e What
f Where
g When
h Who
i When or Where
j What

Page 28

I Make sure the letters are of a regular size, with the a and i joined with a smooth curve. Make sure the letters are sitting on the line.

II Make sure the letters are of a regular size, with the a and r, and the u and n joined with a smooth curve. Make sure the letters are sitting on the line.

Page 29

I Make sure the letters are of a regular size, and that the horizontal joins are carefully written.

II Make sure the letters are of a regular size, and that the horizontal joins are carefully written.

Page 30

I Make sure the taller letter is joined to the small letter correctly. Ensure the letters sit on the lines.

II Make sure the taller letter is joined to the small letter correctly. Ensure the letters sit on the lines.

Page 31

I Make sure the letters are of a regular size, and are joined with a smooth curve. Make sure the letters are sitting on the line.

II Make sure the letters are of a regular size, and are joined with a smooth curve. Make sure the letters are sitting on the line.

Test 1 Letter patterns

Some **letter patterns** are very common.

I can **see** my t**ea**.   I can **row** a b**oa**t.

Choose ee or ea to complete each word.

1. s__ee__d

2. h__ea__t

3. k__ee__p

4. t__ea__ch

5. f__ea__st

b c
bach

Choose oa or ow to complete each word.

6. l__oa__f

7. l__oa__d
coach

8. c____ch

9. sh__ow__

narrow
o

10. narr____

Colour in your score

Test 2 Word order

We have to write words in the **correct order** so they make **sense**.

eat Monkeys bananas. ☒

Monkeys eat bananas. ☑

Write these sentences correctly.

1. milk. Cats drink _____

2. lay eggs. Birds _____

3. asleep. is dog The _____

4. balloon A pop. can _____

5. is The green. grass _____

6. A hop. frog can _____

7. red. My is coat best _____

8. swim pool. You a in _____

9. wash a You sink. in _____

10. tree tall. very The is _____

Colour in your score

Test 3 Adding ing and ed

We can add **ing** and **ed** to the end of some words.

Yesterday I walk**ed** to school.

Today I am walk**ing** to the shops.

**Write these words so they end in ing.
Spell them correctly.**

1. miss _____

2. shop _____

3. write _____

4. carry _____

5. crash _____

**Write these words so they end in ed.
Spell them correctly.**

6. beg _____

7. blame _____

8. copy _____

9. splash _____

10. rub _____

School Shop

10
9
8
7
6
5
4
3
2
1

Colour in your score

Test 3

Test 4 Vowels and consonants

There are **26** letters in the **alphabet**. The five **vowels** are **a, e, i, o** and **u**. All the other letters are called **consonants**.

a	b	c	d	**e**	f	g	h	**i**	j	k	l	m
n	**o**	p	q	r	s	t	**u**	v	w	x	y	z

Every word usually has **at least one** vowel in it.

Fill in the missing vowel in each word.

1. d____ll

2. sh____ll

3. h____ss

4. sn____p

5. d____ck

6. s____nd

7. k____ng

8. m____sk

9. pr____m

10. sh____e

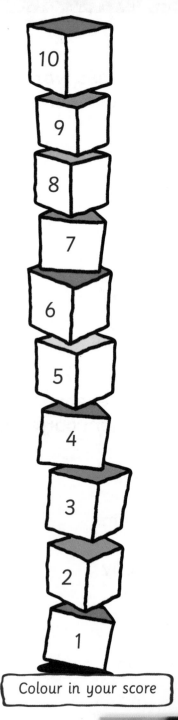

10
9
8
7
6
5
4
3
2
1

Colour in your score

Test 4

Test 5 Making sense of sentences

Sentences must **make sense** when you read them.

The aeroplane flied in the sky. ☒

The aeroplane flew in the sky. ☑

Choose the correct word to finish each sentence.

1. The dog _____ the postman. (bit/bited)

2. The boy _____ the window. (breaked/broke)

3. I _____ the ball. (catched/caught)

4. I _____ the moon. (seed/saw)

5. The girl _____ reading. (is/are)

6. The children _____ running. (was/were)

7. My mum _____ home. (come/came)

8. I _____ in the shop. (went/goed)

9. I _____ got an apple. (has/have)

10. The boy _____ himself. (hurt/hurted)

Colour in your score

Test 5

Test 6 Conjunctions

A **conjunction** is a **joining** word. It may be used to join **two sentences** together.

A mouse is small. An elephant is big.

A mouse is small **but** an elephant is big.

Choose the conjunction and or but to fill each gap.

1. I picked up the apple _____ ate it.

2. The girl found her bag _____ went to school.

3. I got the sum right _____ Ben didn't.

4. The lion stopped _____ roared.

5. I like swimming _____ reading.

6. I sat down _____ watched TV.

7. This door is open _____ that door is shut.

8. Metal is hard _____ wool is soft.

9. I got undressed _____ went to bed.

10. I opened my bag _____ took out a book.

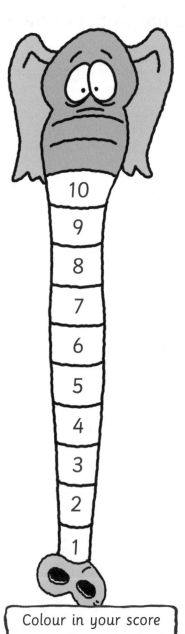

10
9
8
7
6
5
4
3
2
1

Colour in your score

Test 6

Test 7 Rhyming

Rhyming is important in spelling.

I found a pound on the ground.

I **found** a p**ound** on the gr**ound**.

	look	stew	night	
past	head	light	took
	last	new	bread	

Write the five pairs of rhyming words.

1. _____   2. _____

3. _____   4. _____

5. _____   6. _____

7. _____   8. _____

9. _____   10. _____

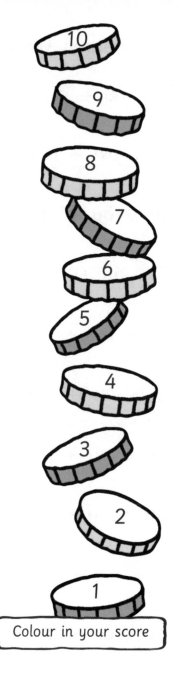

Colour in your score

Test 8 **Word building**

In spelling we have to learn to **build** up words.

h + ow + l = howl

Do these sums. Write the words you make.

1. l + ou + d = _____

2. d + ow + n = _____

3. m + ou + th = _____

4. f + ou + nd = _____

5. cr + ow + d = _____

6. cl + ow + n = _____

7. sh + ou + t = _____

8. sp + ou + t = _____

9. fl + ow + er = _____

10. cr + ou + ch = _____

Colour in your score

Test 8

Test 9 Full stops and question marks

I live in a house.

Where do you live?

A **sentence** often ends with a **full stop**.

A **question** always ends with a **question mark**.

Rewrite each sentence correctly.

1. a farmer lives on a farm _____

2. why are you late _____

3. bees live in a hive _____

4. what is the matter _____

5. where is my pen _____

6. the fox ran quickly _____

7. the clouds were black _____

8. who is your friend _____

9. the wind is blowing _____

10. how did you do it _____

10
9
8
7
6
5
4
3
2
1

Colour in your score

Test 9

Test 10 Putting words in groups

Sometimes it is helpful to put words into **groups**.

Things that give light

torch   sun   candle   lamp   lantern

Sort these words into groups.

tea	beech	elm	water	oak
ash	coffee	cola	yew	juice

Different sorts of drinks.

1. _____

2. _____

3. _____

4. _____

5. _____

Different sorts of trees.

6. _____

7. _____

8. _____

9. _____

10. _____

Colour in your score

Test 10

Test 11 Antonyms

Antonyms are words that are **opposite** in meaning.

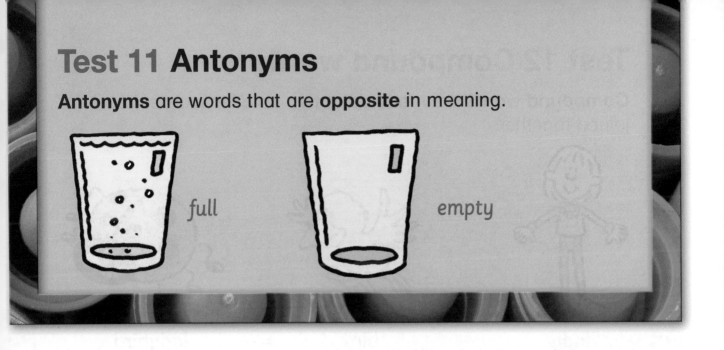

full

empty

Choose the word that means the opposite.

bad	wet	hard	rich	sad
smooth	small	dirty	hot	narrow

1. dry   _____

2. poor   _____

3. cold   _____

4. rough   _____

5. easy   _____

6. wide   _____

7. clean   _____

8. good   _____

9. big   _____

10. happy   _____

Colour in your score

Test 12 Compound words

Compound words are made up of **two smaller words** joined together.

lady   +   bird   =   ladybird

Do the word sums and write the answers.

1. foot + ball = _____

2. rain + bow = _____

3. sun + shine = _____

4. snow + man = _____

5. play + time = _____

6. butter + fly = _____

7. bull + dog = _____

8. hedge + hog = _____

9. black + berry = _____

10. key + hole = _____

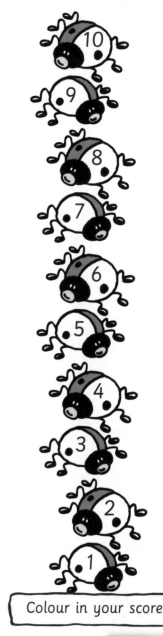

Colour in your score

Test 12

Test 13 Looking carefully at words

We can make new words by **changing some letters**.

cake

rake   sh ake   lake

Write the new words you make.

1. Change the **f** in **f**air to **ch**. _____

2. Change the **r** in **r**are to **fl**. _____

3. Change the **t** in **t**ear to **b**. _____

4. Change the **l** in **l**ord to **c**. _____

5. Change the **j** in **j**aw to **cl**. _____

6. Change the **c** in **c**ore to **sh**. _____

7. Change the **w** in **w**ire to **f**. _____

8. Change the **p** in **p**ure to **c**. _____

9. Change the **f** in **f**ind to **w**. _____

10. Change the **r** in **r**oar to **s**. _____

Colour in your score

Test 13

Test 14 Speech marks

Speech marks show someone is speaking. We write everything the person says **inside** the speech marks.

I deliver letters.

The postman said,

"I deliver letters."

Put in the missing speech marks.

1. The builder said, I use a hammer.

2. The driver said, I drive a big lorry.

3. Mrs Smith said, I am feeling tired.

4. The librarian said, I work in a library.

5. The farmer said, I keep cows on my farm.

6. The queen said, I wear a crown.

7. The nurse said, I work in a hospital.

8. The fire-fighter said, My job is dangerous.

9. The caretaker said, I keep the school clean.

10. The baker said, I make bread.

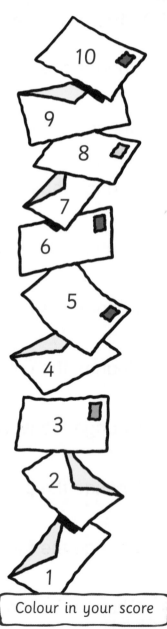

Colour in your score

Test 14

Test 15 The letters wh and ph

Two common letter patterns are **wh** and **ph**.

whistle   dol**ph**in

Choose wh or ph to complete each word.

1. ele_____ant

2. _____ere

3. al_____abet

4. _____eat

5. _____ich

6. gra_____

7. ne_____ew

8. _____iskers

9. _____ite

10. _____antom

Colour in your score

Test 15

Test 16 Syllables

When you say a word slowly you can hear that it can be **broken down** into **smaller chunks** called **syllables**.

drag – on

(two syllables)

Tap out the syllables when you say each word.

Say these words slowly.
Does each word have two or three syllables?

1. elephant _____

2. phantom _____

3. slowly _____

4. syllable _____

5. alphabet _____

6. hairdresser _____

7. drummer _____

8. watering _____

9. inside _____

10. replied _____

Colour in your score

Test 17 Verbs

Verbs tell us what someone is **doing**.

MOO!

A cow **moos**.

Choose the best verb to complete each sentence.

moos   clucks   purrs   neighs   hoots
grunts   gobbles   bleats   quacks   barks

1. A cow _____.

2. An owl _____.

3. A hen _____.

4. A duck _____.

5. A turkey _____.

6. A horse _____.

7. A dog _____.

8. A sheep _____.

9. A pig _____.

10. A cat _____.

Colour in your score

Test 18 Beginnings and endings

Always make sure your **sentences make sense**.

Sam has forgotten to finish her sentence.

Ben has rubbed out the beginning of his sentence.

My pencil...

... watched television.

Join up the beginning and ending of each sentence.

1. The farmer   in the stable.

2. The horse was   are cold.

3. Some birds   drives a tractor.

4. My pencil   is shut.

5. Ice-creams   were singing in the tree.

6. In my garden   is curly.

7. The door   is sharp.

8. I am eating   I grow flowers.

9. My hair   is on.

10. The television   some chips.

Colour in your score

Test 19 The letters er, ir and ur

The letter patterns **er**, **ir** and **ur** make a similar sound.

fern   shirt   purse

Choose er, ir or ur to complete each word.

1. d_____ty

2. k_____b

3. t_____n

4. sh_____t

5. s_____ve

6. n_____se

7. c_____ve

8. st_____

9. b_____d

10. t_____m

Colour in your score

Test 20 Checking your sentences

Always check your writing to see if you have made any silly mistakes.

goes
The rocket ~~go~~ fast.

Choose the correct word to complete each sentence.

1. My uncle _____ very nice. (is/are)

2. The birds _____ very noisy. (was/were)

3. The children _____ reading. (is/are)

4. The girl _____ asleep. (was/were)

5. The cat _____ milk. (like/likes)

6. I _____ it well. (did/does)

7. My cousin _____ to visit. (comed/came)

8. I _____ my shirt. (teared/tore)

9. Tom always _____ hard at maths. (try/tries)

10. Lions _____. (roar/roars)

Colour in your score

Test 20

Test 21 Looking for letter patterns

The letter pattern **ea** has two sounds.

I can r**ea**d a book.

ea sounds like **ee**
(as in r**ee**d)

Yesterday I r**ea**d a comic.

ea sounds like **e**
(as in red)

Divide these words into sets.

| seat | cheat | ready | sweat | feather |
| head | bread | teach | meal | clean |

Write the words in which **ea** sounds like **ee** as in r**ee**d.

1. _____

2. _____

3. _____

4. _____

5. _____

Write the words in which **ea** sounds like **e** as in red.

6. _____

7. _____

8. _____

9. _____

10. _____

Colour in your score

Test 21

Test 22 Commas

Commas are used to **separate** things in a **list**.
We **don't** use a comma before the word **and**.

sheep, duck, pig and hen

Fill in the missing commas.

1. red yellow blue and green

2. lion tiger cheetah and leopard

3. apples pears bananas and grapes

4. pen pencil crayon and felt-tip

5. rain sun snow and fog

6. I saw a car a bus a lorry and a bike.

7. In my bag I took a mirror a ruler and
   a pencil.

8. I like oranges peaches cherries and
   melons.

9. I can play football cricket rugby and
   snooker.

10. A gardener needs a spade a fork a
    trowel and a hoe.

10
9
8
7
6
5
4
3
2
1

Colour in your score

Test 22

Test 23 Adding to the ends of words

Sometimes we can change words by **adding letters** to the **end** of them.

The kitten likes to **play**. It is very play**ful**.

When **full** comes at the end of a word we spell it **ful**.

Do these word sums. Write the answers.

1. use + ful = _____

2. hope + ful = _____

3. help + ful = _____

4. pain + ful = _____

5. thank + ful = _____

Take off ful. Write the word you are left with.

6. colourful _____

7. faithful _____

8. truthful _____

9. cheerful _____

10. careful _____

Colour in your score

Test 23

Test 24 Questions

A **question** should begin with a **capital letter** and end with a **question mark**.

What is this?

Write each question correctly.

1. who looks after our teeth

   _____

2. what flies in the sky

   _____

3. where is your shirt

   _____

4. what do we use to dig with

   _____

5. who lives next door to you

   _____

6. where do we get milk from

   _____

7. why are you crying

   _____

8. how did you do that

   _____

9. who is your best friend

   _____

10. what makes a seed grow

    _____

Colour in your score

Test 25 Exclamation marks

We use an **exclamation mark** when we feel **strongly** about something.

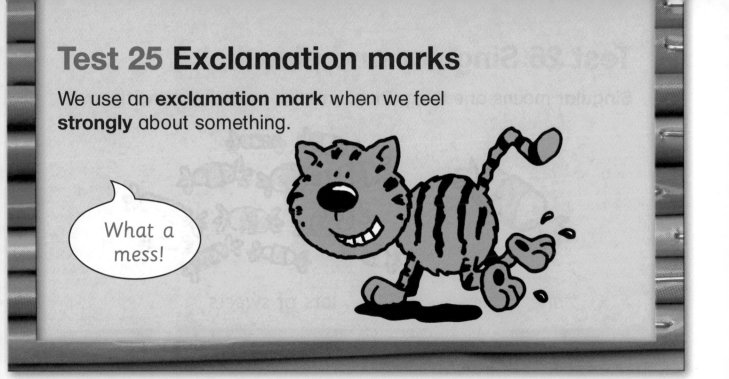

What a mess!

Rewrite each sentence. End each sentence with either a question mark or an exclamation mark.

1. come quickly _____

2. who are you _____

3. when did you arrive _____

4. stop messing about _____

5. what a nice surprise _____

6. what are you doing _____

7. you are horrible _____

8. this cake tastes good _____

9. why are you so upset _____

10. shut that door _____

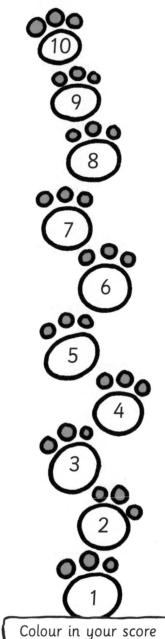

Colour in your score

Test 25

Test 26 Singular and plural

Singular means **one** thing. **Plural** means **more** than one thing.

one sweet   lots of sweets

Complete each of these.

1. one rabbit, lots of _____

2. one chocolate, lots of _____

3. one tree, lots of _____

4. one cap, lots of _____

5. one chair, lots of _____

6. one _____ , lots of plates

7. one _____ , lots of horses

8. one _____ , lots of cakes

9. one _____ , lots of rockets

10. one _____ , lots of dragons

Colour in your score

Test 27 Capital letters

We use a capital letter to **begin** the names of **people**, the names of **days of the week** and **months of the year**.

My name is Shanaz.

My birthday is in March.

Write and spell correctly, the name of some months.

The name of the months begining with J.

1. _____   2. _____

3. _____

The name of the months ending with ber.

4. _____   5. _____

6. _____   7. _____

The name of the months begining with A.

8. _____   9. _____

The name of the month begining with F.

10. _____

Colour in your score

Test 27

Test 28 Synonyms

Synonyms are words with **similar meanings**.

I'm **quick**.

I'm *fast*.

Write the word that has a similar meaning.

damp	upset	closed	dislike	talk
bored	large	go	high	difficult

1. big _____

2. hate _____

3. speak _____

4. leave _____

5. angry _____

6. tall _____

7. fed up _____

8. shut _____

9. wet _____

10. hard _____

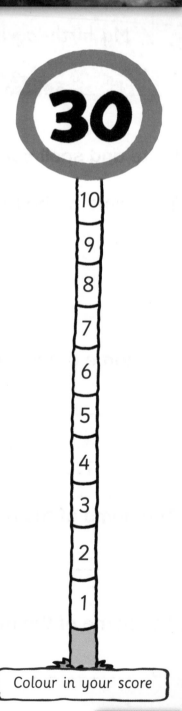

Colour in your score

Test 28

Test 29 Collecting words

We can **group** some words together because they are all **related**.

shirt   jeans   jumper   coat

These are all names of **clothes**.

Underline the odd word out in each group.

1. cricket football book swimming

2. pen arm leg head

3. potato carrot onion sun

4. bridge table chair wardrobe

5. rabbit drums trumpet guitar

6. car bus lorry library

7. daisy bluebell grasshopper buttercup

8. oak bite ash lime

9. telephone London Cardiff Glasgow

10. sheep lion cow hen

Colour in your score

Test 30 Checking up on punctuation

Punctuation marks make writing **easier** to read.

It's raining.

Sam said It's raining ☒

Sam said, "It's raining." ☑

**Fill in all the missing punctuation marks
in these sentences.**

1. The boy got up

2. Where is my dinner

3. Get out of my way

4. I love maths science reading and sports.

5. May I come with you

6. My dog is black

7. Anna said, I'm hungry

8. What a horrible day

9. My bike has a flat tyre, Tom said.

10. How many questions are there

10

9

8

7

6

5

4

3

2

1

Colour in your score

Test 30

ANSWERS

Test 1
The missing letters are in **bold**.
1. s**ee**d
2. h**ea**t
3. k**ee**p
4. te**a**ch
5. fe**a**st
6. lo**a**f
7. lo**a**d
8. co**a**ch
9. sh**ow**
10. narr**ow**

Test 2
1. Cats drink milk.
2. Birds lay eggs.
3. The dog is asleep.
4. A balloon can pop.
5. The grass is green.
6. A frog can hop.
7. My best coat is red.
8. You swim in a pool.
9. You wash in a sink.
10. The tree is very tall.

Test 3
1. missing
2. shopping
3. writing
4. carrying
5. crashing
6. begged
7. blamed
8. copied
9. splashed
10. rubbed

Test 4
The missing vowel is in **bold**.
1. d**o**ll
2. sh**e**ll
3. h**i**ss
4. sn**a**p
5. d**u**ck
6. s**a**nd
7. k**i**ng
8. m**a**sk
9. pr**a**m
10. sh**o**e

Test 5
1. bit
2. broke
3. caught
4. saw
5. is
6. were
7. came
8. went
9. have
10. hurt

Test 6
1. and
2. and
3. but
4. and
5. and
6. and
7. but
8. but
9. and
10. and

Test 7
1. look
2. took
3. stew
4. new
5. night
6. light
7. past
8. last
9. head
10. bread

Test 8
1. loud
2. down
3. mouth
4. found
5. crowd
6. clown
7. shout
8. spout
9. flower
10. crouch

Test 9
1. A farmer lives on a farm.
2. Why are you late?
3. Bees live in a hive.
4. What is the matter?
5. Where is my pen?
6. The fox ran quickly.
7. The clouds were black.
8. Who is your friend?
9. The wind is blowing.
10. How did you do it?

Test 10
1. tea
2. water
3. coffee
4. cola
5. juice
6. beech
7. elm
8. oak
9. ash
10. yew

Test 11
1. wet
2. rich
3. hot
4. smooth
5. hard
6. narrow
7. dirty
8. bad
9. small
10. sad

Test 12
1. football
2. rainbow
3. sunshine
4. snowman
5. playtime
6. butterfly
7. bulldog
8. hedgehog
9. blackberry
10. keyhole

Test 13
1. chair
2. flare
3. bear
4. cord
5. claw
6. shore
7. fire
8. cure
9. wind
10. soar

Test 14
1. The builder said, "I use a hammer."
2. The driver said, "I drive a big lorry."
3. Mrs Smith said, "I am feeling tired."
4. The librarian said, "I work in a library."
5. The farmer said, "I keep cows on my farm."
6. The queen said, "I wear a crown."
7. The nurse said, "I work in a hospital."
8. The fire-fighter said, "My job is dangerous."
9. The caretaker said, "I keep the school clean."
10. The baker said, "I make bread."

Test 15
The missing letters are in **bold**.
1. ele**ph**ant
2. **where**
3. al**ph**abet
4. **wh**eat
5. **wh**ich
6. gra**ph**
7. nep**h**ew
8. **wh**iskers
9. **wh**ite
10. **ph**antom

Test 16
1. three
2. two
3. two
4. three
5. three
6. three
7. two
8. three
9. two
10. two

Test 17
1. moos
2. hoots
3. clucks
4. quacks
5. gobbles
6. neighs
7. barks
8. bleats
9. grunts
10. purrs

Test 18
1. The farmer drives a tractor.
2. The horse was in the stable.
3. Some birds were singing in the tree.
4. My pencil is sharp.
5. Ice-creams are cold.
6. In my garden I grow flowers.
7. The door is shut.
8. I am eating some chips.
9. My hair is curly.
10. The television is on.

Test 19
The missing letters are in **bold**.
1. d**ir**ty
2. k**er**b
3. t**ur**n
4. sh**ir**t
5. s**er**ve
6. n**ur**se
7. c**ur**ve
8. st**ir**
9. b**ir**d
10. t**er**m

Test 20
1. is
2. were
3. are
4. was
5. likes
6. did
7. came
8. tore
9. tries
10. roar

Test 21
1. seat
2. cheat
3. teach
4. meal
5. clean
6. ready
7. sweat
8. feather
9. head
10. bread

Test 22
1. red, yellow, blue and green
2. lion, tiger, cheetah and leopard
3. apples, pears, bananas and grapes
4. pen, pencil, crayon and felt-tip
5. rain, sun, snow and fog
6. I saw a car, a bus, a lorry and a bike.
7. In my bag I took a mirror, a ruler and a pencil.
8. I like oranges, peaches, cherries and melons.
9. I can play football, cricket, rugby and snooker.
10. A gardener needs a spade, a fork, a trowel and a hoe.

Test 23
1. useful
2. hopeful
3. helpful
4. painful
5. thankful
6. colour
7. faith
8. truth
9. cheer
10. care

Test 24
1. Who looks after our teeth?
2. What flies in the sky?
3. Where is your shirt?
4. What do we use to dig with?
5. Who lives next door to you?
6. Where do we get milk from?
7. Why are you crying?
8. How did you do that?
9. Who is your best friend?
10. What makes a seed grow?

Test 25
1. Come quickly!
2. Who are you?
3. When did you arrive?
4. Stop messing about!
5. What a nice surprise!
6. What are you doing?
7. You are horrible!
8. This cake tastes good!
9. Why are you so upset?
10. Shut that door!

Test 26
1. rabbits
2. chocolates
3. trees
4. caps
5. chairs
6. plate
7. horse
8. cake
9. rocket
10. dragon

Test 27
1. January
2. June
3. July
4. September
5. October
6. November
7. December
8. April
9. August
10. February

Test 28
1. large
2. dislike
3. talk
4. go
5. upset
6. high
7. bored
8. closed
9. damp
10. difficult

Test 29
1. book
2. pen
3. sun
4. bridge
5. rabbit
6. library
7. grasshopper
8. bite
9. telephone
10. lion

Test 30
1. The boy got up.
2. Where is my dinner?
3. Get out of my way!
4. I love maths, science, reading and sports.
5. May I come with you?
6. My dog is black.
7. Anna said, "I'm hungry."
8. What a horrible day!
9. "My bike has a flat tyre," Tom said.
10. How many questions are there?

Make it easy...

Maths

with Quick Tests

Age 6-7

Numbers to 20

The numbers between 12 and 20 are **teen** numbers.

They all end in **...teen**.

11 and 12 are made from a ten and ones, but do not end in **teen**.

13 → thirteen

10 + 3 = 13

I Write the words or numbers for each of these.

a 15 →

b 18 →

c 11 →

d 17 →

e fourteen →

f nineteen →

g twelve →

h sixteen →

II Write the word for each number.

a 13 →

b 12 →

c 18 →

d 17 →

e 14 →

f 19 →

The hidden number in the shaded area is ☐.

2

Counting

Use this grid to help you learn the **order** of numbers to 50.

1	2	3	4	5	6	7	8	9	10
11	12	13	14	15	16	17	18	19	20
21	22	23	24	25	26	27	28	29	30
31	32	33	34	35	36	37	38	39	40
41	42	43	44	45	46	47	48	49	50

I Fill in the missing numbers.

a   27 28 ☐ ☐ ☐ 32 ☐ 34 ☐ ☐

b   ☐ ☐ ☐ 43 44 ☐ ☐ ☐ 48 49

c   ☐ ☐ 29 ☐ 27 26 ☐ ☐ 23 22

d   ☐ ☐ 48 ☐ ☐ 45 44 43 ☐ ☐

e   16 ☐ ☐ ☐ 20 ☐ 22 ☐ 24 ☐

II These are all part of the 1–50 grid. Use the grid at the top of the page to help fill in the missing numbers.

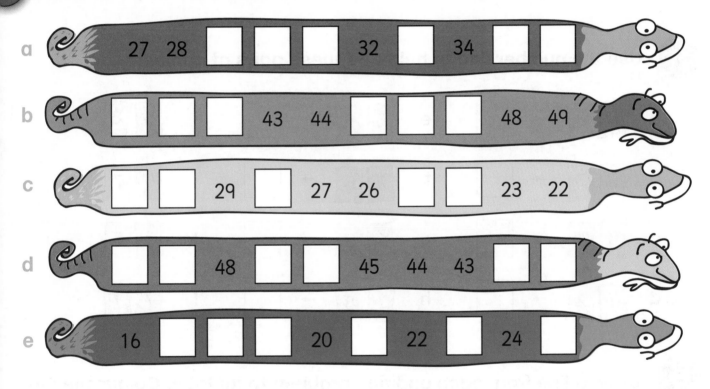

a

	☐		
14		☐	
☐	26	28	
35	☐		
☐			

b

22	☐		☐	
32	33		36	
☐		44		

c

☐	☐		10
	18		☐
☐		38	40
☐			

Adding

A **number line** can help with addition.

What is 4 + 7?

0 1 2 3 4 5 6 7 8 9 10 11 12 13 14 15 16 17 18 19 20

Start with the biggest number and count on.

7 + 4 = 11

I Use the number line to help add these pairs of numbers.

a 6 3 → ☐   e 6 6 → ☐   i 3 8 → ☐

b 5 7 → ☐   f 9 5 → ☐   j 6 7 → ☐

c 8 4 → ☐   g 4 9 → ☐   k 8 5 → ☐

d 7 2 → ☐   h 7 8 → ☐   l 7 7 → ☐

II Draw a line from each addition problem to its total. Colour the star with no matching fact.

a 3 + 9   e 8 + 8   g 7 + 3   i 10 + 9

c 7 + 7   f 7 + 6   j 6 + 5

b 9 + 9   d 9 + 6

h 10 + 10

☆10 ☆11 ☆12 ☆13 ☆14 ☆15 ☆16 ☆17 ☆18 ☆19 ☆20

2-D shapes

A 2-D shape is a **flat shape**.

Learn the names and number of sides of these shapes.

| triangle | quadrilateral | pentagon | hexagon | heptagon | octagon |
| 3 sides | 4 sides | 5 sides | 6 sides | 7 sides | 8 sides |

Rectangles and squares are special quadrilaterals.

I Draw lines to join the shapes to the correct name.

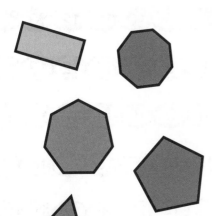

triangle

rectangle

pentagon

hexagon

heptagon

octagon

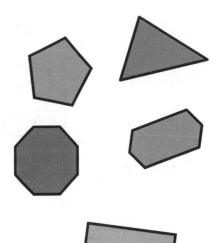

II Colour this stained glass window using the colour code below.

 triangles

 quadrilaterals

 pentagons

5

Taking away

You can count back along a number line to help you **subtract**, or **take away**.

What is 14 – 5? Start at 14 and count back 5.

0 1 2 3 4 5 6 7 8 9 10 11 12 13 14 15

14 – 5 = 9

I Show the jumps for each subtraction. Then write the answer in the box.

a 11 – 4 = ☐   ①②③④⑤⑥⑦⑧⑨⑩⑪⑫⑬⑭⑮

b 13 – 5 = ☐   ①②③④⑤⑥⑦⑧⑨⑩⑪⑫⑬⑭⑮

c 12 – 7 = ☐   ①②③④⑤⑥⑦⑧⑨⑩⑪⑫⑬⑭⑮

d 16 – 7 = ☐   ⑥⑦⑧⑨⑩⑪⑫⑬⑭⑮⑯⑰⑱⑲⑳

e 18 – 6 = ☐   ⑥⑦⑧⑨⑩⑪⑫⑬⑭⑮⑯⑰⑱⑲⑳

f 17 – 6 = ☐   ⑥⑦⑧⑨⑩⑪⑫⑬⑭⑮⑯⑰⑱⑲⑳

II Make each subtraction match the number on the stars.

a

10 – ☐

☐ – 2

6

12 – ☐

☐ – 3

☐ – 8

b

11 – ☐

☐ – 7

7

9 – ☐

☐ – 6

15 – ☐

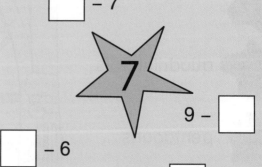

Numbers to *100*

This grid shows the numbers to 100.

Use the **tens** to help you read and write the numbers.

20 twenty	60 sixty
30 thirty	70 seventy
40 forty	80 eighty
50 fifty	90 ninety

1	2	3	4	5	6	7	8	9	10
11	12	13	14	15	16	17	18	19	20
21	22	23	24	25	26	27	28	29	30
31	32	33	34	35	36	37	38	39	40
41	42	43	44	45	46	47	48	49	50
51	52	53	54	55	56	57	58	59	60
61	62	63	64	65	66	67	68	69	70
71	72	73	74	75	76	77	78	79	80
81	82	83	84	85	86	87	88	89	90
91	92	93	94	95	96	97	98	99	100

I **Circle the correct number for each of these.**

a thirty-eight   83   37   78   38   30

b fifty-four   44   50   46   45   54

c seventy-nine   97   17   79   76   96

d sixty-two   52   26   60   62   80

e eighty-seven   81   78   80   76   87

II **Find these numbers on the word search. They are written across → and down ↓.**

20	60
30	70
40	80
50	90

T	W	E	N	T	Y	E	F
N	S	I	X	T	Y	F	I
I	Y	G	N	H	V	O	F
N	E	H	E	Y	I	R	T
E	S	T	H	I	R	T	Y
T	R	Y	M	L	F	Y	E
Y	S	E	V	E	N	T	Y

Addition and subtraction

This **number trio** can make 4 addition and subtraction facts.

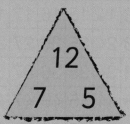

7 + 5 = 12   12 − 7 = 5

5 + 7 = 12   12 − 5 = 7

I Fill in the addition and subtraction facts for these.

a

```
5 + ☐ = ☐

☐ + 5 = ☐

☐ − 5 = ☐

☐ − ☐ = 5
```

b

```
☐ + ☐ = 15

☐ + 6 = 15

15 − ☐ = ☐

15 − ☐ = ☐
```

c

```
9 + ☐ = ☐

☐ + 9 = ☐

☐ − ☐ = 9

☐ − 9 = ☐
```

II Choose 8 different numbers from the line below to complete these facts.

⭐1 ⭐2 ⭐3 ⭐4 ⭐5 ⭐6 ⭐7 ⭐8 ⭐9

 4 + ☐ = ⭐9   7 − ⭐5 = ☐   ⭐8 − ☐ = ⭐1

☐ + ☐ = ⭐11   ⭐12 − ☐ = ⭐8   ☐ + ⭐3 = ☐

8

Counting patterns

Practise **counting on** and **back** in steps of 2, 5 and 10.

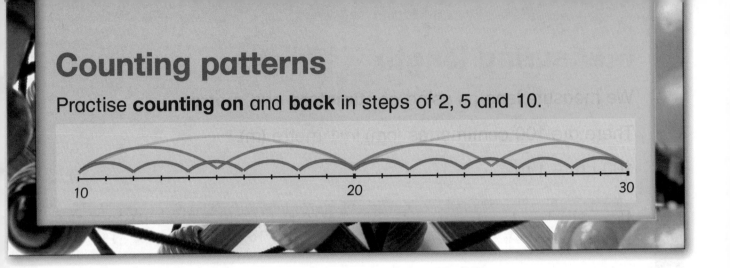

I Continue each of these counting patterns to 100. Mark them on the 100 square like this:

2 4 6 8 10 12 → 100

5 10 15 20 25 → 100

10 20 30 40 50 → 100

1	2	3	4	5	6	7	8	9	10
11	12	13	14	15	16	17	18	19	20
21	22	23	24	25	26	27	28	29	30
31	32	33	34	35	36	37	38	39	40
41	42	43	44	45	46	47	48	49	50
51	52	53	54	55	56	57	58	59	60
61	62	63	64	65	66	67	68	69	70
71	72	73	74	75	76	77	78	79	80
81	82	83	84	85	86	87	88	89	90
91	92	93	94	95	96	97	98	99	100

II Count in **5s** and fill in the next 4 numbers.

a   4   9

b   22   27

c   43   48

Now count in **10s** and fill in the next 4 numbers.

d   8   18

e   27   37

f   39   49

Measuring length

We measure lengths using **centimetres** and **metres**.

There are 100 centimetres (cm) in 1 metre (m).

100 cm = 1 m

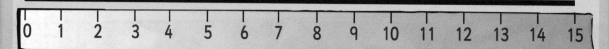

This line shows 15 cm.

I Use a ruler to measure each of these lengths in centimetres.

a _____ [ ] cm

b _____ [ ] cm

c _____ [ ] cm

d ___ [ ] cm

e _____ [ ] cm

f _____ [ ] cm

Try estimating the length before you measure.

II Draw lines to join these objects to the most likely length.

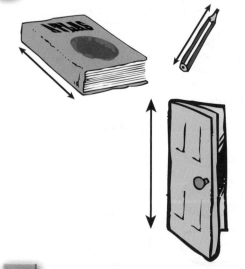

about 1 metre

about 2 metres

about 10 centimetres

more than 2 metres

about 50 cm

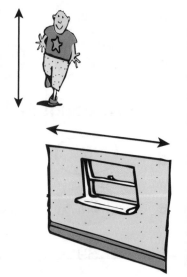

Finding totals

When you add together 3 or more numbers, try **starting** with the **largest number**.

Here's how to total 4, 3 and 8:

$$8 + 4 = 12$$

$$12 + 3 = 15$$

You could look for pairs that are easy to total.

Here's how to total 6, 5 and 4:

$$6 + 4 = 10$$

$$10 + 5 = 15$$

I Fill in the totals for these sets of additions.

a 6 2 8 → ☐

d 9 1 8 → ☐

g 8 4 6 → ☐

b 5 2 9 → ☐

e 7 3 4 → ☐

h 3 3 8 → ☐

c 7 2 3 → ☐

f 5 9 5 → ☐

i 4 6 3 → ☐

II Make these totals in different ways.

a 4 + ☐ + ☐

☐ + ☐ + 5

☐ + 6 + ☐

13

☐ + 3 + ☐

8 + ☐ + ☐

☐ + ☐ + 1

b ☐ + ☐ + 9

☐ + 6 + ☐

7 + ☐ + ☐

18

4 + ☐ + ☐

☐ + 8 + ☐

☐ + ☐ + 5

11

Odd and even numbers

Even numbers always end in

2 4 6 8 0

36
is an even number.

Odd numbers always end in

1 3 5 7 9

63
is an odd number.

I **Write the next even number.**

a 22 →

b 38 →

c 46 →

d 60 →

e 54 →

Write the next odd number.

f 35 →

g 57 →

h 29 →

i 87 →

j 91 →

II **Colour red the even number trail. Start at the IN gate.**

OUT

19	24	32	48	85	33	34	26	18	70	96	73	34	26	14
23	6	61	16	51	27	58	35	43	19	34	85	58	21	43
42	30	25	40	10	7	94	65	24	46	52	17	92	80	19
85	27	41	93	28	43	62	97	12	21	33	29	31	52	21
17	35	43	8	32	76	44	81	16	54	36	28	56	74	45

IN

How many stars have you collected?

12

3-D shapes

A 3-D shape is a **solid shape**.

Learn the names of these shapes. Look at the faces.

square face

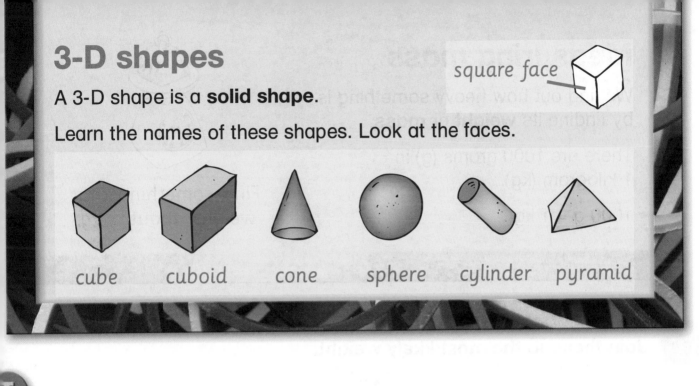

cube   cuboid   cone   sphere   cylinder   pyramid

I Draw lines to join each shape to its correct name.

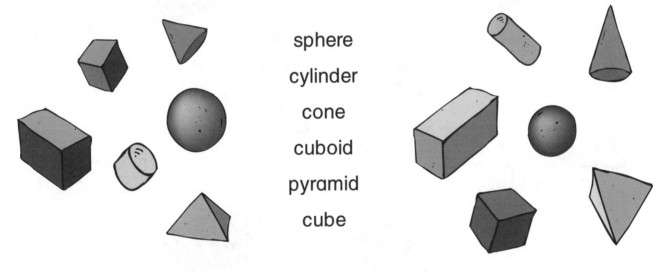

sphere

cylinder

cone

cuboid

pyramid

cube

II Fill in the number of faces for each of these shapes.

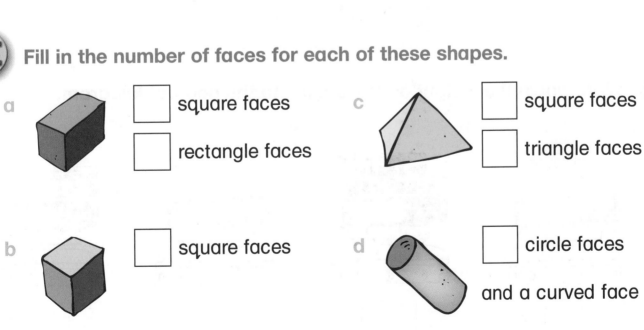

a
☐ square faces

☐ rectangle faces

c
☐ square faces

☐ triangle faces

b
☐ square faces

d
☐ circle faces

and a curved face

13

Measuring mass

We find out how heavy something is by finding its **weight** or **mass**.

There are 1000 grams (g) in 1 kilogram (kg).

1000 g = 1 kg

Find something that weighs about 1 kg.

I   Join these to the most likely weight.

II   Write down the weight on the scales to the nearest kilogram.

a   b   c   d

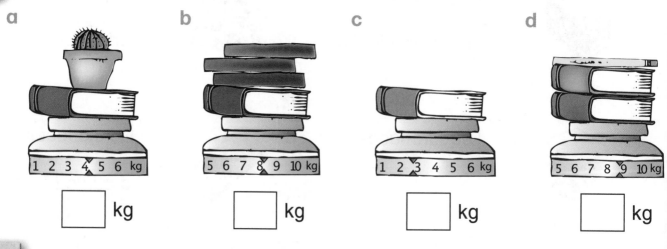

☐ kg   ☐ kg   ☐ kg   ☐ kg

Breaking up numbers

The numbers between **10** and **99** all have **two digits**.

$$57 \rightarrow 50 + 7$$

5 tens   7 ones

I Fill in the missing numbers.

a 34 → 30 + ☐

b 51 → ☐ + 1

c 47 → 40 + ☐

d 65 → ☐ + 5

e 83 → 80 + ☐

f 42 → ☐ + 2

g 29 → 20 + ☐

h 76 → ☐ + 6

i 59 → 50 + ☐

II Draw lines to join the matching pairs.

53

34

35

Reading the time

These clocks show **quarter past eight**.

8:15

15 minutes have gone past 8 o'clock.

These clocks show **quarter to five**.

4:45

45 minutes have gone past 4 o'clock.

 Draw lines to join the clocks showing the same time.

a    b   c   d   e   f   g

| 11:30 | 3:00 | 1:15 | 12:45 | 6:45 | 4:15 | 7:15 |

 Write the number of minutes between each of these times.

a ☐ minutes

c 10:45 11:00 ☐ minutes

b  ☐ minutes

d 3:15 3:45 ☐ minutes

Multiplying

Counting in equal groups is also called **multiplying**.

The multiplication sign is **×**.

3 + 3 + 3 + 3 = 12

4 lots of 3 is 12

4 × 3 = 12

4 + 4 + 4 = 12

3 lots of 4 is 12

3 × 4 = 12

These both give the same answer.

 Write the answers to these facts.

a   2 + 2 + 2 = ☐

   3 × 2 = ☐

d   4 + 4 = ☐

   2 × 4 = ☐

b    5 + 5 = ☐

   2 × 5 = ☐

e   3 + 3 + 3 = ☐

   3 × 3 = ☐

c   3 + 3 + 3 + 3 + 3 = ☐

   5 × 3 = ☐

f   4 + 4 + 4 + 4 = ☐

   4 × 4 = ☐

 Draw 2 spots on each hat.
Then write the answer.

Draw 3 spots on each hat.
Then write the answer.

a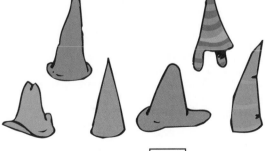

b

6 × 2 = ☐

6 × 3 = ☐

Symmetrical shapes

Shapes are **symmetrical** if they are the same either side of a **mirror line**.

The mirror line is called the **line of symmetry**.

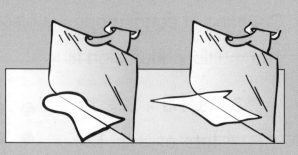

I Draw a line of symmetry on each of these shapes.

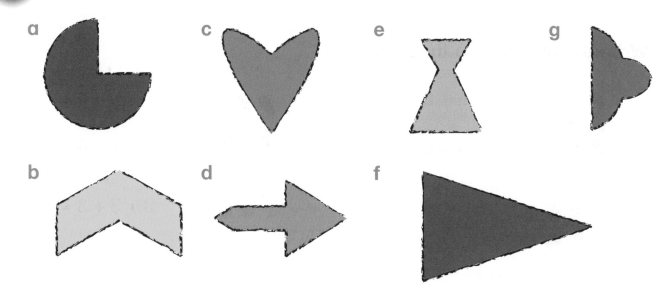

a

c

e

g

b

d

f

II Complete this to make a symmetrical shape. Then colour it to make a symmetrical pattern.

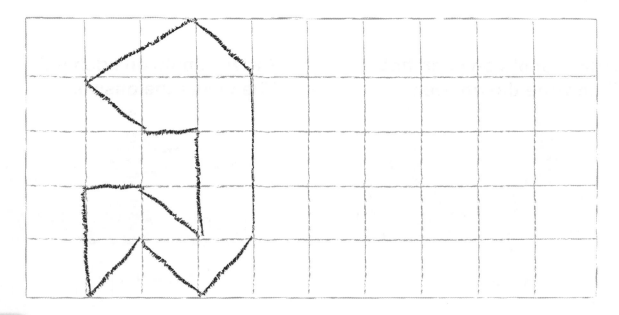

Ordering numbers

When you put **2-digit** numbers in order, look at the **tens and then the ones** digit.

52 is larger than 38 because 5 tens is more than 3 tens.

Use this number line to help.

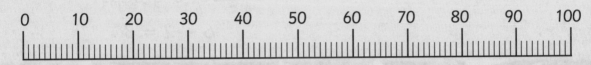

0   10   20   30   40   50   60   70   80   90   100

I Write a number in each box so there are four numbers in order.

a  42 ▷ ▷ ▷ 50 ▷

b 61 ▷ ▷ ▷ 73 ▷

c 57 ▷ ▷ ▷ 64 ▷

d  82 ▷ ▷ ▷ 91 ▷

e 66 ▷ ▷ ▷ 71 ▷

f 76 ▷ ▷ ▷ 83 ▷

g  94 ▷ ▷ ▷ 98 ▷

h 88 ▷ ▷ ▷ 92 ▷

i 57 ▷ ▷ ▷ 61 ▷

II Write these sets in order, starting with the smallest amount.

a  58p 39p 85p 42p 61p

☐ p ☐ p ☐ p ☐ p ☐ p

b 73 kg 69 kg 37 kg 39 kg 76 kg

☐ kg ☐ kg ☐ kg ☐ kg ☐ kg

c 32 cm 23 cm 80 cm 38 cm 28 cm

☐ cm ☐ cm ☐ cm ☐ cm ☐ cm

d £53 £62 £29 £65 £35

£☐ £☐ £☐ £☐ £☐

Dividing

Dividing a number of objects can be shown by grouping them.

The division sign is ÷.

6 beans grouped in twos, gives 3 groups

$$6 \div 2 = 3$$

 Draw loops around these beans to group them. Write the answers.

a 8 grouped in 2s

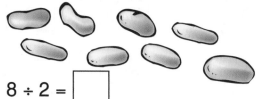

8 ÷ 2 = ☐

c 12 grouped in 3s

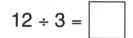

12 ÷ 3 = ☐

b 9 grouped in 3s

9 ÷ 3 = ☐

d 10 grouped in 2s

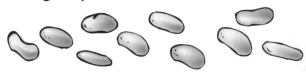

10 ÷ 2 = ☐

 Use the cookies to help you complete these.

a

15 ÷ 5 = ☐

c

10 ÷ 2 = ☐

b

15 ÷ 3 = ☐

d

10 ÷ 5 = ☐

Reading graphs

Block graphs show information in a simple way.

Count the blocks carefully or read across for the amount.

A group of children threw 10 beanbags trying to get them into a bucket.

How many more beanbags did Zoe get in than Fred?

A group of children tested how many pegs they could hold in one hand.

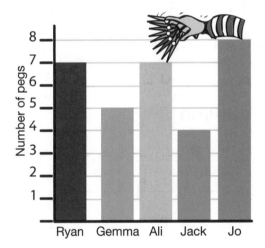

a Who held the most pegs?

b How many pegs did Gemma hold?

c Which 2 children held the same number of pegs?

d Who held the fewest pegs?

e How many more pegs did Jo hold than Jack?

Carry out your own peg test. Ask family and friends to hold as many pegs as they can in one hand. Record your results as a pictogram.

Name	Number of pegs

= 1 peg

Time

There are **12 months** or **52 weeks** in **a year**.

Try to learn the order of the months and the seasons. Think about the month and season you were born in.

 spring   summer   autumn   winter

I **Complete the names of the months for each season.**

spring

M __ __ c h

A __ r __ l

__ __ y

winter

D __ __ __ m b __ __

__ __ n u __ r __

F __ __ r __ __ __ y

summer

J __ __ e

__ __ __ y

A __ __ u __ __

autumn

S __ p __ __ __ __ __ __ r

__ __ t __ b __ __

N __ __ e __ b __ __

II **Complete these time facts.**

a ☐ days in a week

b ☐ months in a year

c ☐ weeks in a year

d ☐ hours in a day

e ☐ minutes in an hour

f ☐ seconds in a minute

g ☐ days in a fortnight

h ☐ days in a weekend

i ☐ seasons in a year

j ☐ months in a season

2 times table

The numbers in the **2 times table** can be shown as a pattern.

Try to learn the 2 times table by heart.

$1 \times 2 = 2$

$2 \times 2 = 4$

Draw lines to join the questions to the correct answers.

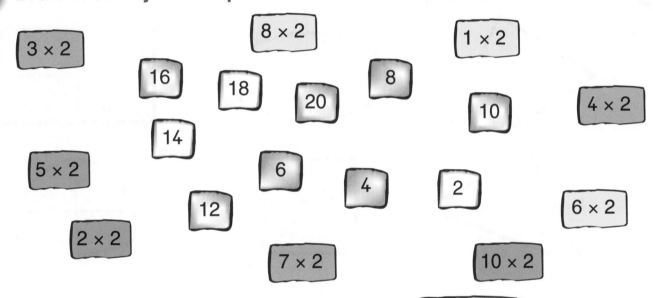

a Write a calculation for the answer that is left.

Answer these questions as fast as you can. Ask someone to time you.

a $3 \times 2 = \boxed{}$

$7 \times 2 = \boxed{}$

$4 \times 2 = \boxed{}$

$1 \times 2 = \boxed{}$

$6 \times 2 = \boxed{}$

b $2 \times 10 = \boxed{}$

$2 \times 2 = \boxed{}$

$2 \times 8 = \boxed{}$

$2 \times 5 = \boxed{}$

$2 \times 9 = \boxed{}$

c $8 \times 2 = \boxed{}$

$2 \times 6 = \boxed{}$

$9 \times 2 = \boxed{}$

$2 \times 7 = \boxed{}$

$5 \times 2 = \boxed{}$

Half fractions

This chocolate bar is cut into **2 equal pieces.**

Each piece is **half ($\frac{1}{2}$)** of the whole bar.

There are 8 squares of chocolate.

$\frac{1}{2}$ of 8 = 4

I Colour $\frac{1}{2}$ of each shape.

a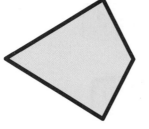

c

e

b

d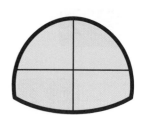

f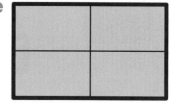

II Circle $\frac{1}{2}$ of each set. Write the answer.

a  $\frac{1}{2}$ of 6 = ☐

c     $\frac{1}{2}$ of 10 = ☐

b  $\frac{1}{2}$ of 8 = ☐

d $\frac{1}{2}$ of 4 = ☐

Measuring capacity

The **capacity** of a jug shows how much **liquid** it holds.

> 1000 millilitres (ml) = 1 litre (l)

Fill a 1 litre jug so that you know how much a litre is.

 Draw lines to join these things to the most likely amount.

less than 1 litre	greater than 1 litre

 **Write down these amounts to the nearest litre.**

a

☐ litres

c

☐ litres

e

☐ litres

b

☐ litres

d

☐ litres

f

☐ litres

Money

Practise finding totals of **coins** and giving **change**. When you give change, try counting up.

A cake costs 39p. Think about the change you will get from 50p.

Count on from 39p to 50p.

+1p   +10p

39p   40p   50p

The change is 11p.

I Draw the 3 coins you would use to buy each of these.

a  ○○○

d  ○○○

b  ○○○

e  ○○○

c  ○○○

f  ○○○

II This is the change given from 50p. How much did each cake cost?

a

cost ➜ ☐ p

b

cost ➜ ☐ p

c

cost ➜ ☐ p

Number sequences

This sequence counts on in **steps of 2**.

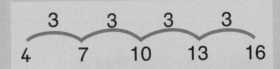

5 6 **7** 8 **9** 10 **11** 12 **13** 14 **15**

The difference between each number is 2.

When you are writing sequences of numbers, look at the **difference** between each number.

	3	3	3	3
4	7	10	13	16

I) Write the next 2 numbers in each sequence.

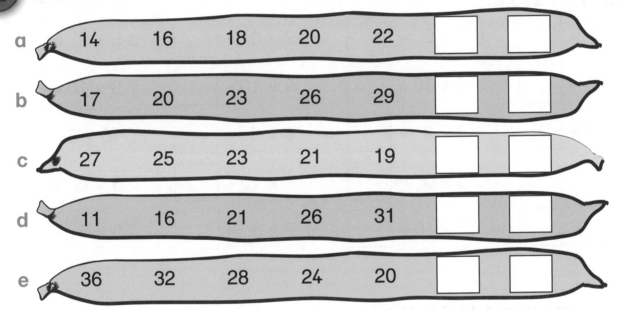

a 14   16   18   20   22   ☐   ☐

b 17   20   23   26   29   ☐   ☐

c 27   25   23   21   19   ☐   ☐

d 11   16   21   26   31   ☐   ☐

e 36   32   28   24   20   ☐   ☐

II) Write 3 sequences of your own. The number 20 must be in each sequence.

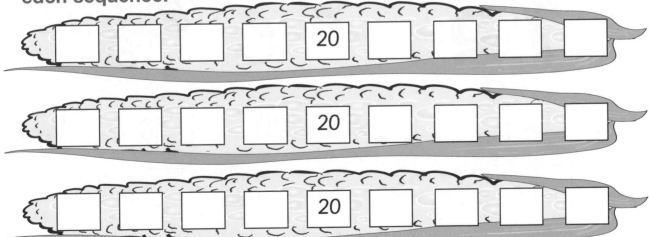

☐ ☐ ☐ ☐ 20 ☐ ☐ ☐ ☐

☐ ☐ ☐ ☐ 20 ☐ ☐ ☐ ☐

☐ ☐ ☐ ☐ 20 ☐ ☐ ☐ ☐

Multiplication facts

Try to learn the **2** times,
5 times and **10** times tables.

Use this grid to help you.

×	1	2	3	4	5	6	7	8	9	10
2	2	4	6	8	10	12	14	16	18	20
5	5	10	15	20	25	30	35	40	45	50
10	10	20	30	40	50	60	70	80	90	100

I Cover the grid above. Now answer these questions as fast as you can. Check your answers, then try to beat your score.

a 3 × 5 = ☐   b 4 × 2 = ☐   c 2 × 2 = ☐   d 5 × 2 = ☐

6 × 2 = ☐   7 × 10 = ☐   9 × 10 = ☐   8 × 10 = ☐

4 × 10 = ☐   9 × 2 = ☐   6 × 5 = ☐   10 × 5 = ☐

8 × 2 = ☐   5 × 5 = ☐   2 × 10 = ☐   3 × 2 = ☐

4 × 5 = ☐   3 × 10 = ☐   7 × 5 = ☐   9 × 5 = ☐

II Write the digits 1 to 9 in the boxes to make each sum correct.

2 × ☐ = ☐   ☐ × 5 = 20   ☐0 × ☐ = 80

☐ × ☐ = 35   ☐ × ☐ = 18

☐ × ☐ = 40

Quarter fractions

This cake is cut into **4 equal pieces**.

Each piece is **one quarter ($\frac{1}{4}$)** of the whole cake.

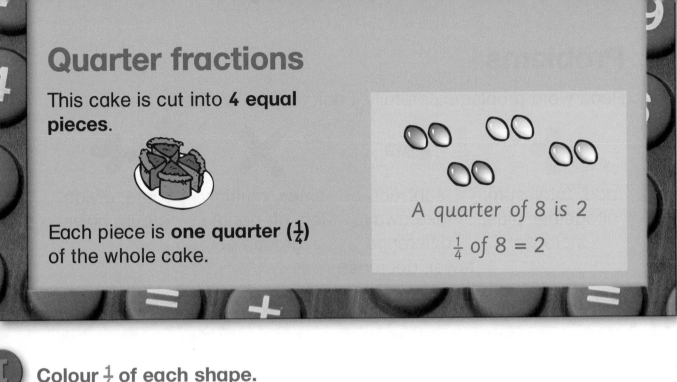

A quarter of 8 is 2

$\frac{1}{4}$ of 8 = 2

I Colour $\frac{1}{4}$ of each shape.

a

c

e

b

d

f

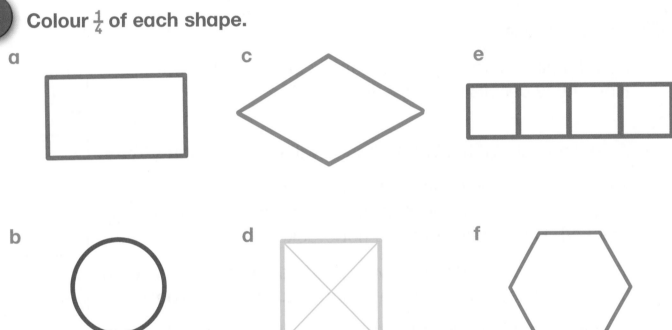

II Colour $\frac{1}{4}$ of the ribbons on these badges. Make sure each pattern is different.

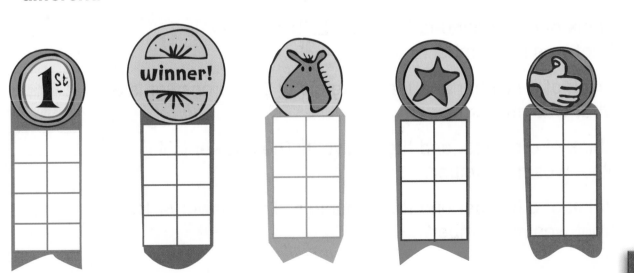

Problems

Read word problems carefully. Look for **key words** to help you.

| add, total, sum, altogether, plus, increase | subtract, take away, difference, fewer, decrease | times, multiply, lots of, double, groups of | share, divide, group, halve |

I Answer these problems.

a Four friends share 20 pencils equally between them. How many pencils do they each have?

b A T-shirt costs £3.50. What change will there be from £5?

c Tom buys 2 boxes of eggs with 6 eggs in each. When he gets home he finds that 3 eggs are cracked. How many eggs are not cracked?

d When a tree was planted, it was 2 metres high. After 5 years it was 10 times as high. What height was it after 5 years?

e Entrance to a fête costs 40p for adults and 10p for children. What is the total cost for a family of 2 adults and 3 children?

II Answer these 'think of a number' puzzles.

a I think of a number and then add 2. The answer is 7. What was my number?

b I think of a number and then take away 5. The answer is 6. What was my number?

c I think of a number and then halve it. The answer is 4. What was my number?

d I think of a number and then double it. The answer is 10. What was my number?

Finding the difference

To find the **difference** between 2 numbers, count on from the smaller number.

What is the difference between 19 and 23?

19   20   21   22   23   24   25   23 – 19 = 4

I Write the difference in price between these pairs of items.

a

Difference: £ [ ]

c

Difference: £ [ ]

e

Difference: £ [ ]

b

Difference: £ [ ]

d

Difference: £ [ ]

f

Difference: £ [ ]

II Draw lines to join pairs with a difference of 6.

68

56

75

62

83

94

74

88   81   77

Page 2

I a fifteen e 14
b eighteen f 19
c eleven g 12
d seventeen h 16

II a thirteen d seventeen
b twelve e fourteen
c eighteen f nineteen
The hidden number is 11

Page 3

I a 29, 30, 31, 33, 35, 36
b 40, 41, 42, 45, 46, 47
c 31, 30, 28, 25, 24
d 50, 49, 47, 46, 42, 41
e 17, 18, 19, 21, 23, 25

II a

	5				
14	15		17		
24	25	26	27	28	29
	35	36	37	38	
	45	46			

b

22	23		25	26
32	33	34	35	36
42		44	45	

c

6	7	8		10
		18	19	20
		28	29	30
	37	38	39	40
			49	50

Page 4

I a 9 e 12 i 11
b 12 f 14 j 13
c 12 g 13 k 13
d 9 h 15 l 14

II a 12 e 16 i 19
b 18 f 13 j 11
c 14 g 10
d 15 h 20
17 is the star coloured in.

Page 5

I

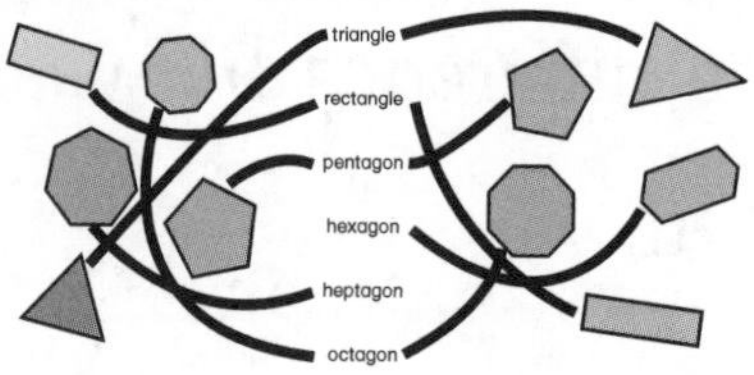

II Check your child's colouring is accurate.

Page 6

I a 7 c 5 e 12
b 8 d 9 f 11

II a 8 – 2, 10 – 4, 12 – 6, 14 – 8, 9 – 3
b 14 – 7, 11 – 4, 9 – 2, 15 – 8, 13 – 6

Page 7

I a 38 c 79 e 87
b 54 d 62

II

T	W	E	N	T	Y	E	F
N	S	I	X	T	Y	F	I
I	Y	G	N	H	V	O	F
N	E	H	E	Y	I	R	T
E	S	T	H	I	R	T	Y
T	R	Y	M	L	F	Y	E
Y	S	E	V	E	N	T	Y

Page 8

I a 5 + 8 = 13 13 – 5 = 8
8 + 5 = 13 13 – 8 = 5
b 6 + 9 = 15 15 – 9 = 6
9 + 6 = 15 15 – 6 = 9
c 9 + 8 = 17 17 – 8 = 9
8 + 9 = 17 17 – 9 = 8

II 4 + 5 = 9 12 – 4 = 8
8 + 3 = 11 8 – 7 = 1
7 – 5 = 2 6 + 3 = 9

Page 9

I

1	2	3	4	5	6	7	8	9	10
11	12	13	14	15	16	17	18	19	20
21	22	23	24	25	26	27	28	29	30
31	32	33	34	35	36	37	38	39	40
41	42	43	44	45	46	47	48	49	50
51	52	53	54	55	56	57	58	59	60
61	62	63	64	65	66	67	68	69	70
71	72	73	74	75	76	77	78	79	80
81	82	83	84	85	86	87	88	89	90
91	92	93	94	95	96	97	98	99	100

II a 14, 19, 24, 29
b 32, 37, 42, 47
c 53, 58, 63, 68
d 28, 38, 48, 58,
e 47, 57, 67, 77
f 59, 69, 79, 89

Page 10

I a 5 cm c 8 cm e 10 cm
b 6 cm d 2 cm f 11 cm

II about 1 metre – child
about 2 metres – door
about 10 cm – pencil
more than 2 metres – wall
about 50 cm – book

Page 11

I a 16 d 18 g 18
b 16 e 14 h 14
c 12 f 19 i 13

II a There are many possible solutions, check your child's additions total 13.
b There are many possible solutions, check your child's additions total 18.

Page 12

I a 24 e 56 i 89
b 40 f 37 j 93
c 48 g 59
d 62 h 31

II

19	24	32	48	85	33	34	26	18	70	96	73	34	26	14
23	6	61	16	51	27	58	35	43	19	34	85	58	21	43
42	30	25	40	10	7	94	65	24	46	52	17	92	80	19
85	27	41	93	28	43	62	97	12	21	33	29	31	52	21
17	35	43	8	32	76	44	81	16	54	36	28	56	74	45

10 stars were collected.

Page 13

I

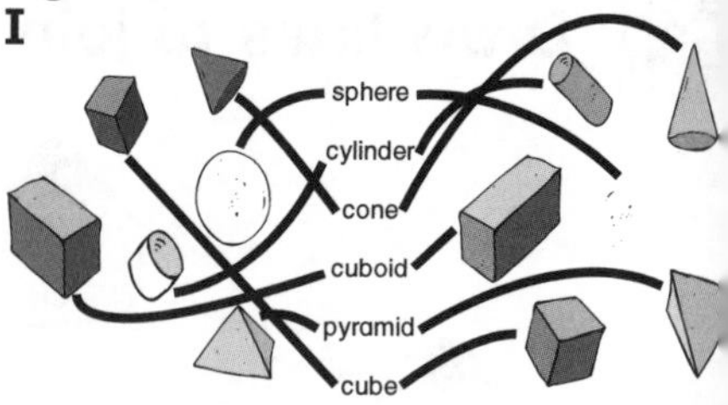

II a 2 square faces, 4 rectangle faces
b 6 square faces
c 1 square face, 4 triangle faces
d 2 circle faces and a curved face

Page 14

I Less than 1 kg – biscuits, grapes, slipper, crisps
More than 1 kg – dog, potatoes, multi-pack of beans, encyclopedia

II **a** 4 kg   **c** 3 kg
     b 8 kg   **d** 9 kg

Page 15

I **a** 4   **d** 60   **g** 9
     b 50   **e** 3   **h** 70
     c 7   **f** 40   **i** 9

II

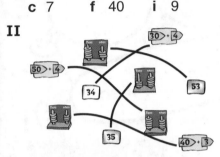

Page 16

I **a** 1.15   **d** 7.15   **g** 4.15
     b 6.45   **e** 12.45
     c 11.30 **f** 3.00

II **a** 30 minutes
     b 45 minutes
     c 15 minutes
     d 30 minutes

Page 17

I **a** 6, 6   **d** 8, 8
     b 10, 10   **e** 9, 9
     c 15, 15   **f** 16, 16

II **a** 12   **b** 18

Page 18

I **a** ... **c** ... **e** ... **g** ...
     b ... **d** ... **f** ...

II

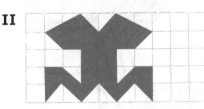

Page 19

I Answers can be any 2 numbers, in order, between:
     a 42 and 50   **f** 76 and 83
     b 61 and 73   **g** 94 and 98
     c 57 and 64   **h** 88 and 92
     d 82 and 91   **i** 57 and 61
     e 66 and 71

II **a** 39p, 42p, 58p, 61p, 85p
     b 37 kg, 39 kg, 69 kg, 73 kg, 76 kg
     c 23 cm, 28 cm, 32 cm, 38 cm, 80 cm
     d £29, £35, £53, £62, £65

Page 20

I **a** 4   **b** 3   **c** 4   **d** 5

II **a** 3   **b** 5   **c** 5   **d** 2

Page 21

I **a** Jo   **d** Jack
     b 5   **e** 4
     c Ali and Ryan

II Check your child's graph is accurate.

Page 22

I Spring: March, April, May
Summer: June, July, August
Autumn: September, October, November
Winter: December, January, February

II **a** 7   **e** 60   **h** 2
     b 12   **f** 60   **i** 4
     c 52   **g** 14   **j** 3
     d 24

Page 23

I $3 \times 2 \rightarrow 6$ $4 \times 2 \rightarrow 8$
     $5 \times 2 \rightarrow 10$ $6 \times 2 \rightarrow 12$
     $2 \times 2 \rightarrow 4$ $10 \times 2 \rightarrow 20$
     $8 \times 2 \rightarrow 16$ $7 \times 2 \rightarrow 14$
     $1 \times 2 \rightarrow 2$
     a $9 \times 2 \rightarrow 18$

II **a** 6, 14, 8, 2, 12
     b 20, 4, 16, 10, 18
     c 16, 12, 18, 14, 10

Page 24

I Check your child has halved each shape accurately and coloured one-half. There is more than one solution to some of the shapes.

II **a** 3   **b** 4   **c** 5   **d** 2

Page 25

I Less than 1 litre – glass of squash, cup of tea, medicine bottle, soup bowl
Greater than 1 litre – bottle of drink, fish tank, washing-up bowl, bucket

II **a** 7 litres   **d** 4 litres
     b 9 litres   **e** 2 litres
     c 6 litres   **f** 8 litres

Page 26

I **a** 20p, 20p, 2p
     b 50p, 2p, 1p
     c £1, 10p, 5p
     d 10p, 5p, 1p
     e 50p, 20p, 10p
     f £1, 20p, 20p

II **a** 15p   **b** 33p   **c** 41p

Page 27

I **a** 24, 26   **d** 36, 41
     b 32, 35   **e** 16, 12
     c 17, 15

II Ask your child what the difference is between the numbers in each sequence and check the numbers are correct.

Page 28

I **a** 15, 12, 40, 16, 20
     b 8, 70, 18, 25, 30
     c 4, 90, 30, 20, 35
     d 10, 80, 50, 6, 45

II $2 \times 1 = 2, 2 \times 2 = 4$,
     $2 \times 3 = 6$ or $2 \times 4 = 8$
     $4 \times 5 = 20$
     $10 \times 8 = 80, 20 \times 4 = 80$,
     $40 \times 2 = 80$ or $80 \times 1 = 80$
     $7 \times 5 = 35$ or $5 \times 7 = 35$
     $2 \times 9 = 18, 9 \times 2 = 18$,
     $3 \times 6 = 18$ or $6 \times 3 = 18$
     $5 \times 8 = 40$ or $8 \times 5 = 40$

Page 29

I Check your child has divided each shape accurately into four parts and coloured one-quarter. There is more than one solution to some of the shapes.

II There are many solutions, check only 2 parts of each badge is coloured in.

Page 30

I **a** 5 pencils   **d** 20m
     b £1.50   **e** £1.10
     c 9 eggs

II **a** 5   **c** 8
     b 11   **d** 5

Page 31

I **a** £5   **c** £5   **e** £4
     b £8   **d** £5   **f** £6

II

Test 1 Read and write numbers to 100

Use these numbers to help you.

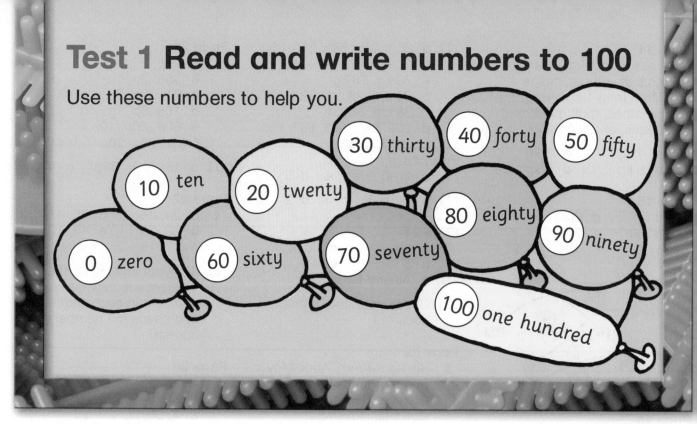

Write the numbers to match the words.

1. thirty-four

2. forty-six

3. twenty-eight

4. seventy-two

5. eighty-nine

Write these numbers as words.

6. 23 _____

7. 56 _____

8. 91 _____

9. 67 _____

10. 49 _____

Colour in your score

Test 1

Test 2 Addition

We use a **number line** to help us **add on**.

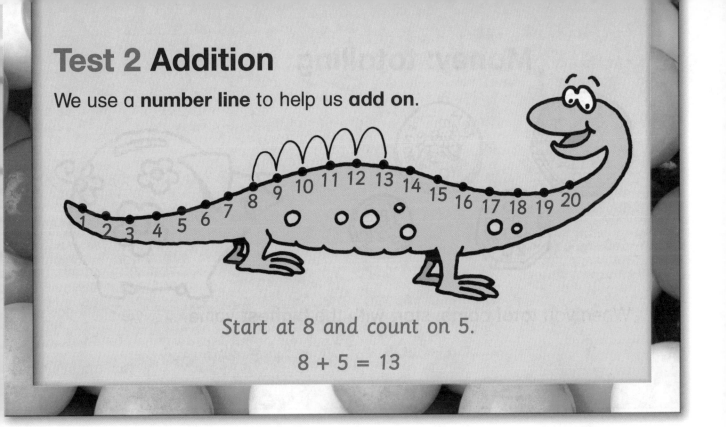

Start at 8 and count on 5.

8 + 5 = 13

Use the number line to help you work out the answers.

1.   6   +   5   =

2. 11   +   3   =

3.   8   +   6   =

4. 12   +   4   =

5.   9   +   5   =

6.   6   +   11   =

7.   7   +   9   =

8.   8   +   4   =

9. 14   +   4   =

10. 13   +   6   =

Colour in your score

Test 2

Test 3 Money: totalling

When you **total coins**, start with the **highest** value.

$$50p + 20p + 10p + 5p = 85p$$

Total each set of coins.

1. (10p) (50p) (2p) ⇨ ☐ p

2. (5p) (2p) (2p) (10p) ⇨ ☐ p

3. (2p) (1p) (20p) (10p) ⇨ ☐ p

4. (20p) (10p) (50p) (2p) ⇨ ☐ p

5. (2p) (5p) (10p) (1p) ⇨ ☐ p

6. (50p) (20p) (2p) (1p) ⇨ ☐ p

7. (20p) (20p) (2p) (10p) (2p) ⇨ ☐ p

8. (2p) (1p) (10p) (5p) (10p) ⇨ ☐ p

9. (50p) (20p) (5p) (10p) (1p) ⇨ ☐ p

10. (2p) (10p) (2p) (5p) (20p) ⇨ ☐ p

Colour in your score

Test 3

Test 4 **2D shapes**

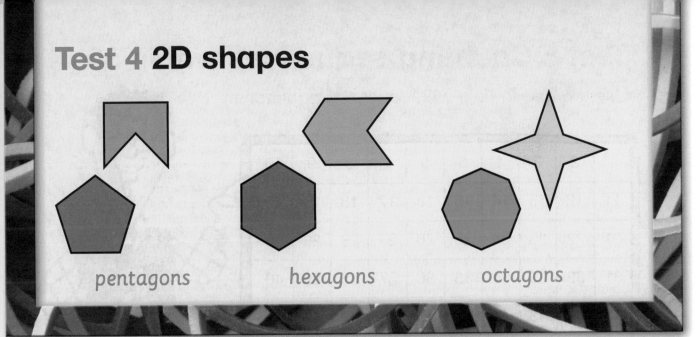

pentagons   hexagons   octagons

Answer these questions.

1. All triangles have ☐ sides.

2. All hexagons have ☐ sides.

3. All pentagons have ☐ sides.

4. All octagons have ☐ sides.

5. All quadrilaterals have ☐ sides.

Name these shapes.

6. _____

7. _____

8. _____

9. _____

10. _____

Colour in your score

Test 4

Test 5 Counting sequences within 50

Use the grid to help with counting sequences.

1	2	3	4	5	6	7	8	9	10
11	12	13	14	15	16	17	18	19	20
21	22	23	24	25	26	27	28	29	30
31	32	33	34	35	36	37	38	39	40
41	42	43	44	45	46	47	48	49	50

Write the missing number in each sequence.

1. 24 25 26 ◯ 28 29

2. 35 36 37 38 ☐ 40

3. ☐ 19 20 21 22 23

4. 41 ☐ 43 44 45 46

5. 28 29 30 31 32 ◯

6. 43 42 41 ☐ 39 38

7. 29 28 ☐ 26 25 24

8. 18 ☐ 16 15 14 13

9. 47 46 45 44 ◯ 42

10. ☐ 39 38 37 36 35

Colour in your score

Test 5

Test 6 Subtraction: finding differences

Counting in jumps can help to find the difference.

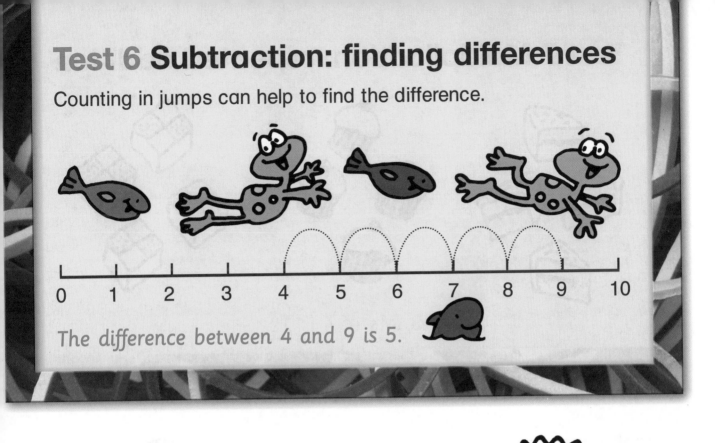

The difference between 4 and 9 is 5.

Write the differences between these pairs of numbers.

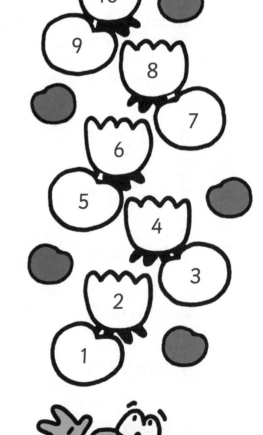

1. 4 7 ☐

6. 12 7 ☐

2. 3 9 ☐

7. 9 11 ☐

3. 5 10 ☐

8. 14 8 ☐

4. 9 2 ☐

9. 13 9 ☐

5. 8 3 ☐

10. 6 11 ☐

Colour in your score

Test 7 Multiplication: repeated addition

3 lots of 4 is 12

Write the answers.

1. 3 lots of 2 ⇨ ☐

2. 2 lots of 4 ⇨ ☐

3. 3 lots of 3 ⇨ ☐

4. 2 lots of 5 ⇨ ☐

5. 4 lots of 3 ⇨ ☐

6. 2 lots of 2 ⇨ ☐

7. 5 lots of 3 ⇨ ☐

8. 3 lots of 5 ⇨ ☐

9. 4 lots of 2 ⇨ ☐

10. 2 lots of 3 ⇨ ☐

Colour in your score

Test 7

Test 8 Division: sharing

These sweets are shared equally.

15 sweets among 3 children ⟹ [5] each.

Write the answers.

1. 12 shared by 2 ⟹ [ ]

2. 8 shared by 4 ⟹ [ ]

3. 6 shared by 3 ⟹ [ ]

4. 10 shared by 2 ⟹ [ ]

5. 9 shared by 3 ⟹ [ ]

6. 12 shared by 3 ⟹ [ ]

7. 10 shared by 5 ⟹ [ ]

8. 6 shared by 2 ⟹ [ ]

9. 12 shared by 4 ⟹ [ ]

10. 8 shared by 2 ⟹ [ ]

10
9
8
7
6
5
4
3
2
1

Colour in your score

Test 9 Time (1)

4.00	1.30	10.15	6.45

Write the times for each clock.
Choose from these times.

1.15	3.30	4.45	8.00	2.30
8.45	3.15	7.30	9.00	4.15

1.

6.

2.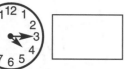

7.

3.

8.

4.

9.

5.

10.

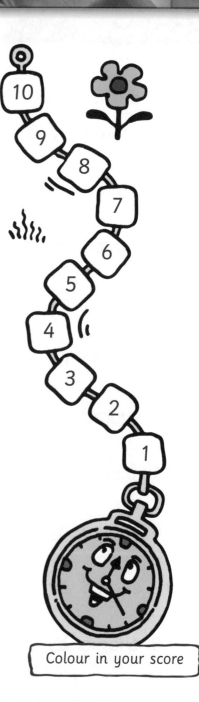

Colour in your score

Test 9

Test 10 Data: block graphs

Colour this **graph** showing the favourite fruit of a group of children.

number of children

6
5
4
3
2
1

apples   oranges   pears   grapes   peaches   bananas

fruit

How many children chose:

1. oranges? ☐

2. grapes? ☐

3. bananas? ☐

4. peaches? ☐

5. Which fruit was the children's favourite? ☐

6. Which fruit was chosen by 3 children? ☐

7. How many more children chose grapes than peaches? ☐

8. How many fewer children chose oranges than bananas? ☐

9. How many children chose pears and peaches altogether? ☐

10. How many children were there altogether? ☐

10
9
8
7
6
5
4
3
2
1

Colour in your score

Test 10

Test 11 Breaking up numbers

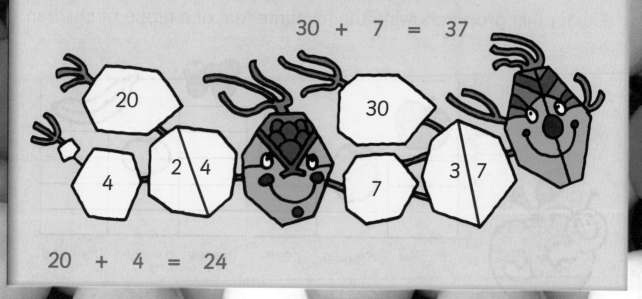

30 + 7 = 37

20 + 4 = 24

Write the missing numbers.

1. 43 = ☐ + 3

2. 56 = 50 + ☐

3. 39 = 30 + ☐

4. 61 = ☐ + 1

5. 27 = ☐ + 7

6. 46 = 40 + ☐

7. 83 = ☐ + 3

8. 74 = ☐ + 4

9. 32 = 30 + ☐

10. 91 = ☐ + 1

Colour in your score

Test 11

Test 12 Subtraction facts

This is a **function machine** for changing numbers.

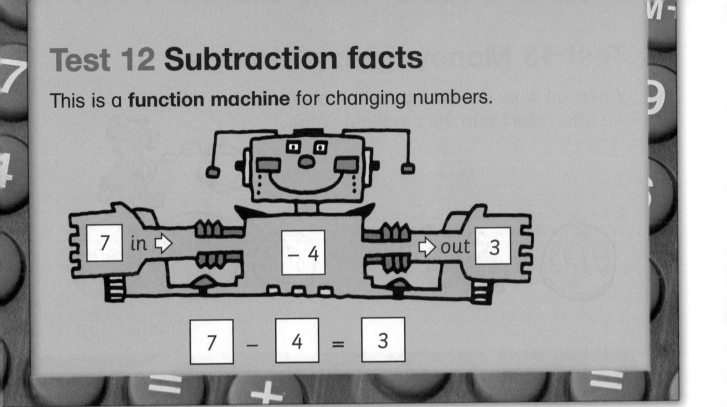

$$7 \quad \text{in} \Rightarrow \qquad -4 \qquad \Rightarrow \text{out} \quad 3$$

$$7 \quad - \quad 4 \quad = \quad 3$$

Write the missing numbers.

1. $8 - \boxed{} = 5$

2. $\boxed{} - 2 = 6$

3. $7 - 3 = \boxed{}$

4. $\boxed{} - 4 = 5$

5. $9 - \boxed{} = 6$

6. $8 - 2 = \boxed{}$

7. $\boxed{} - 3 = 7$

8. $8 - \boxed{} = 3$

9. $6 - \boxed{} = 1$

10. $\boxed{} - 4 = 3$

Colour in your score

Test 13 Money: giving change

When we work out **change** with **coins**, we often **start** with the **smallest value**.

65p

change: 35p

£1 is given for each toy. Write the change given.

1. 85p   ☐ p

2. 70p   ☐ p

3. 55p   ☐ p

4. 60p   ☐ p

5. 80p   ☐ p

6. 45p   ☐ p

7. 75p   ☐ p

8. 89p   ☐ p

9. 78p   ☐ p

10. 67p   ☐ p

Colour in your score

Test 14 3D shapes

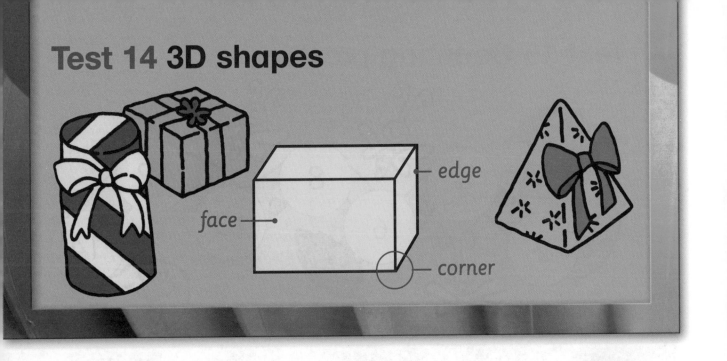

face — edge

corner

Name these shapes.

1.
_____

2.
_____

3.
_____

4.
_____

5.
_____

6.
_____

How many faces have each of these shapes?

7. 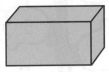 ☐ faces

8. ☐ faces

9. ☐ faces

10. ☐ faces

10
9
8
7
6
5
4
3
2
1

Colour in your score

Test 14

Test 15 Counting patterns

Write the next number in the pattern.

1. (18) (20) (22) (24) (26) ( )

2. [34] [36] [38] [40] [42] [ ]

3. (20) (25) (30) (35) (40) ( )

4. [15] [18] [21] [24] [27] [ ]

5. (8) (12) (16) (20) (24) ( )

Write the missing number.

6. — (14) — [ ] — (18) — (20) — (22) — (24) —

7. — (45) — (40) — (35) — [ ] — (25) — (20) —

8. — (9) — (12) — [ ] — (18) — (21) — (24) —

9. — (28) — (24) — (20) — (16) — [ ] — (8) —

10. — [ ] — (27) — (24) — (21) — (18) — (15) —

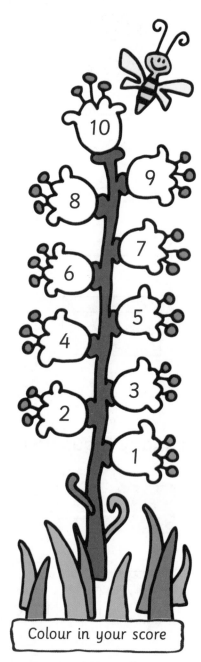

Colour in your score

Test 15

Test 16 Decade sums

Answer these questions.

1. 40 + 20 = ☐

2. 30 + 30 = ☐

3. 30 + 10 = ☐

4. 40 + 60 = ☐

5. 50 + 40 = ☐

6. 20 + 20 = ☐

The three corner numbers add up to 100.
Write the missing number.

7.
10 / 100 / 30 / ○

9.
○ / 100 / 50 / 20

8.
30 / 100 / ○ / 60

10.
○ / 100 / 30 / 20

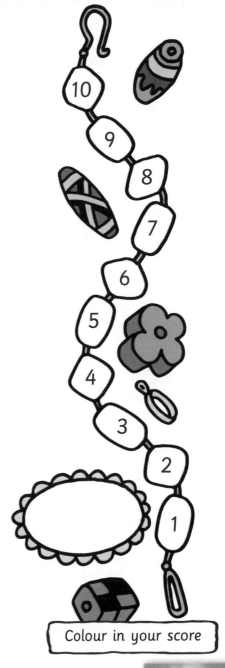

Colour in your score

Test 16

Test 17 2 times table

You need to know your **2 times table**.

How quickly can you answer these?

1. 3 × 2 =

2. 7 × 2 =

3. 2 × 6 =

4. 8 × 2 =

5. 2 × 4 =

6. 2 × 9 =

7. 5 × 2 =

8. 1 × 2 =

9. 10 × 2 =

10. 2 × 2 =

Colour in your score

Test 17

Test 18 Fractions: halves and quarters

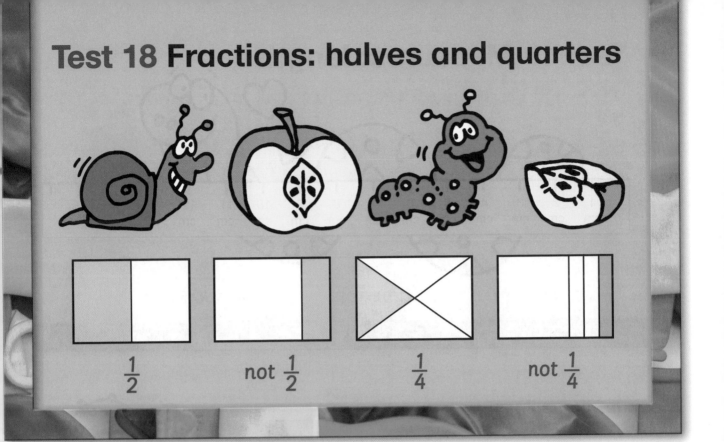

$\frac{1}{2}$ not $\frac{1}{2}$ $\frac{1}{4}$ not $\frac{1}{4}$

Colour $\frac{1}{2}$ of each shape.

1.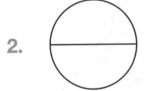

2.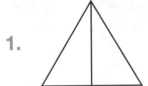

3.

4.

5.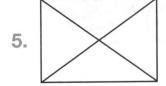

Colour $\frac{1}{4}$ of each shape.

6.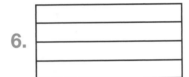

7.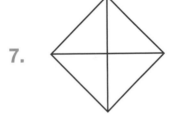

8.

9.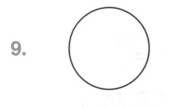

10.

Colour in your score

Test 18

Test 19 Measures: length

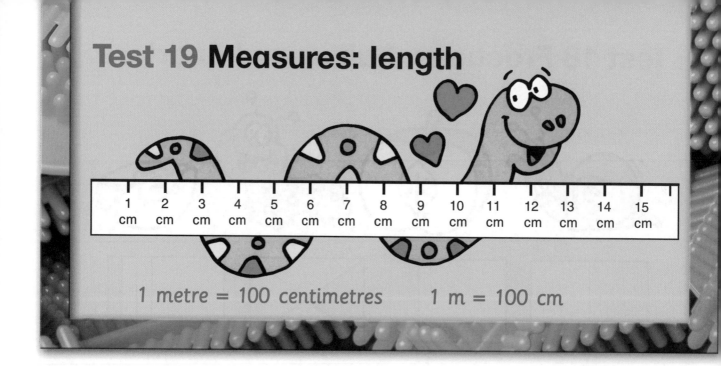

| 1 cm | 2 cm | 3 cm | 4 cm | 5 cm | 6 cm | 7 cm | 8 cm | 9 cm | 10 cm | 11 cm | 12 cm | 13 cm | 14 cm | 15 cm |

1 metre = 100 centimetres   1 m = 100 cm

Measure these lines.

1. _____ ☐ cm

2. _____ ☐ cm

3. _____ ☐ cm

4. _____ ☐ cm

5. _____ ☐ cm

Guess how long each worm is.

6. ☐ cm

7. ☐ cm

8. ☐ cm

9. ☐ cm

10. ☐ cm

10

9

8

7

6

5

4

3

2

1

Colour in your score

Test 19

Test 20 Data: pictograms

This **pictogram** shows the pets owned by a group of children.

dogs	🐕 🐕 🐕 🐕 🐕
cats	🐱 🐱 🐱 🐱 🐱 🐱
rabbits	🐰 🐰 🐰
mice	🐭 🐭 🐭
fish	🐟 🐟 🐟 🐟

How many children have a pet:

1. dog ☐

2. fish ☐

3. mouse ☐

4. rabbit ☐

5. cat ☐

6. How many more cats are there than fish ? ☐

7. How many fewer rabbits are there than dogs? ☐

8. How many mice and cats are there altogether? ☐

9. How many fish and dogs are there altogether? ☐

10. How many pets are there altogether? ☐

Colour in your score

10
9
8
7
6
5
4
3
2
1

Test 20

Test 21 Comparing and ordering numbers

Use this **number line** to help you **compare** and **order numbers**.

0 — 10 — 20 — 30 — 40 — 50

100 — 90 — 80 — 70 — 60

Circle the bigger number in each pair.

1. (46)   (61)   2. 68   (83)

3. 39   (41)   4. (93)   39

5. (57)   54

Write the numbers in order starting with the smallest.

6. (18) (34) (27) (41)

7. (61) (52) (59) (62)

8. (38) (41) (52) (37)

9. (51) (53) (59) (54)

10. (72) (69) (64) (70)

10
9
8
7
6
5
4
3
2
1

Colour in your score

Test 21

Test 22 Addition and subtraction

This **number trio** makes **addition** and **subtraction** facts.

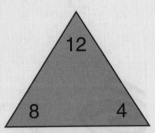

| 8 | + | 4 | = | 12 |

| 4 | + | 8 | = | 12 |

| 12 | − | 4 | = | 8 |

| 12 | − | 8 | = | 4 |

Write the addition and subtraction facts for each of these number trios.

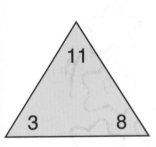

3 + 8 = 11

8 + 3 = 11

1. 11 − ☐ = 8

2. 11 − 8 = ☐

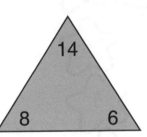

3. 8 + ☐ = 14

4. 6 + ☐ = ☐

5. ☐ − 6 = ☐

6. ☐ − 8 = ☐

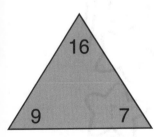

7. ☐ + 7 = ☐

8. ☐ + 9 = ☐

9. 16 − ☐ = ☐

10. ☐ − ☐ = 7

Colour in your score

Test 22

Test 23 Problems

To work out a **missing number** use the other numbers to help you.

$$\boxed{} + 6 = 15$$

Something add 6 equals 15.

$$9 + 6 = 15$$

Write the missing numbers.

1. $\boxed{} + 3 = 11$

2. $6 + \boxed{} = 12$

3. $\boxed{} + 7 = 15$

4. $\boxed{} + 4 = 12$

5. $9 + 6 = \boxed{}$

6. $8 + \boxed{} = 16$

7. $4 + \boxed{} = 11$

8. $\boxed{} + 7 = 10$

9. $5 + 8 = \boxed{}$

10. $9 + \boxed{} = 18$

10
9
8
7
6
5
4
3
2
1

Colour in your score

Test 23

Test 24 Shapes

These shapes have a line of **symmetry**.

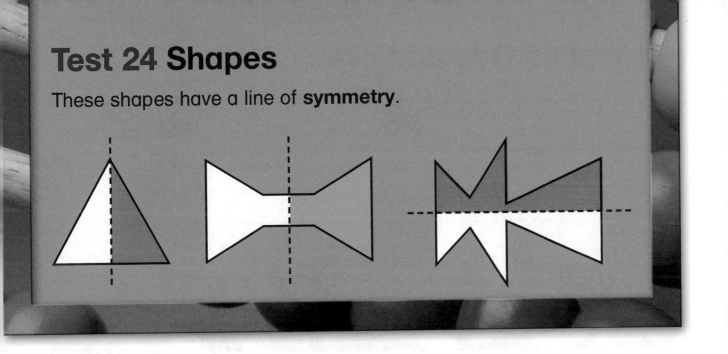

Draw the lines of symmetry on these shapes.

1.

2.

3.

4.

5.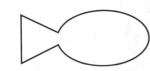

Name these shapes.
Tick them if they are symmetrical.

6.  _____ ☐

7. 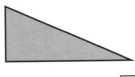 _____ ☐

8. _____ ☐

9. _____ ☐

10.  _____ ☐

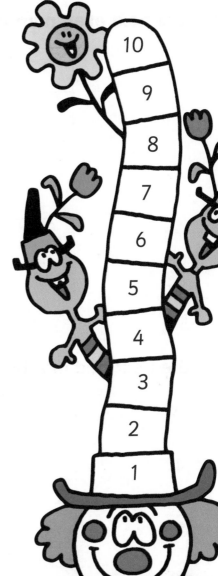

Colour in your score

Test 24

Test 25 Odd and even numbers

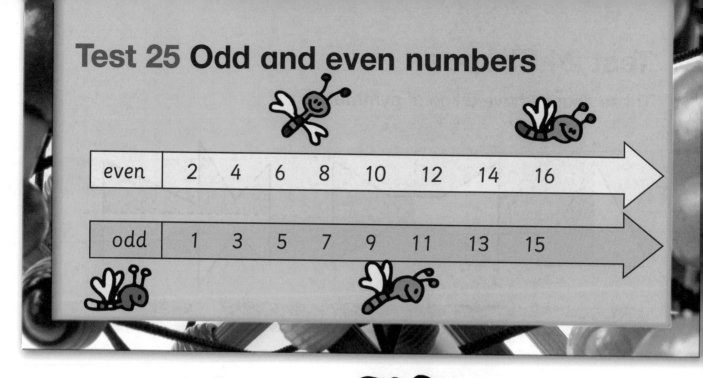

even	2	4	6	8	10	12	14	16
odd	1	3	5	7	9	11	13	15

Write the next even number.

1.   22

2.   28

3.   36

4.   44

5.   40

Write the next odd number.

6.   39

7.   41

8.   27

9.   35

10. 43

10

9

8

7

6

5

4

3

2

1

Colour in your score

Test 25

Test 26 Money and place value

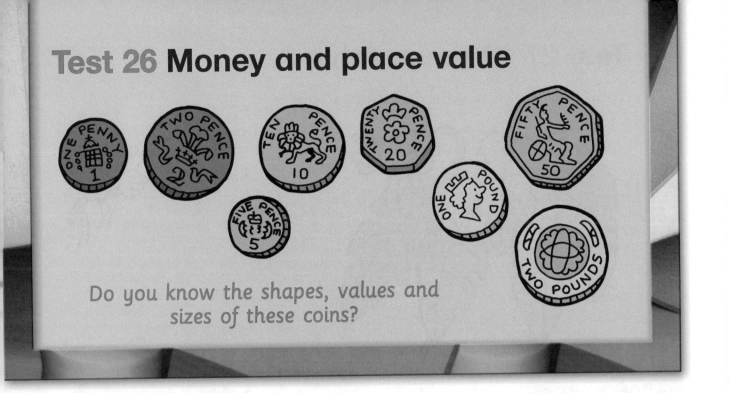

Do you know the shapes, values and sizes of these coins?

Write each of these totals.

1. (20p) (20p) (10p) (£1) ⇨ £ [.   ]

2. (50p) (50p) (20p) (10p) ⇨ £ [.   ]

3. (20p) (20p) (50p) (£1) ⇨ £ [.   ]

4. (£1) (£1) (20p) (10p) ⇨ £ [.   ]

5. (£1) (50p) (20p) (10p) ⇨ £ [.   ]

6. (£1) (£2) (20p) (10p) ⇨ £ [.   ]

7. (10p) (20p) (20p) (£2) ⇨ £ [.   ]

8. (£2) (£2) (50p) (20p) ⇨ £ [.   ]

9. (50p) (50p) (20p) (£2) ⇨ £ [.   ]

10. (20p) (50p) (£1) (£1) ⇨ £ [.   ]

Colour in your score

Test 26

Test 27 10 times table

You need to know your **10 times table**.

How quickly can you answer these?

1. 4 × 10 =

2. 10 × 3 =

3. 7 × 10 =

4. 1 × 10 =

5. 5 × 10 =

6. 10 × 6 =

7. 10 × 2 =

8. 8 × 10 =

9. 10 × 10 =

10. 9 × 10 =

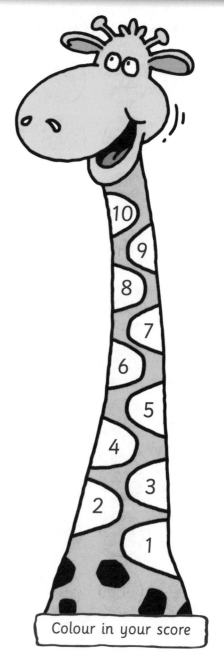

Colour in your score

Test 28 Fractions of quantities

$\frac{1}{2}$ of 4 = 2 $\frac{1}{4}$ of 8 = 2

Find half of each of these.

1.  $\frac{1}{2}$ of 6 = ☐

2.  $\frac{1}{2}$ of 10 = ☐

3.  $\frac{1}{2}$ of 12 = ☐

Work out the answers.

4. $\frac{1}{2}$ of 8 = ☐   8. $\frac{1}{4}$ of 12 = ☐

5. $\frac{1}{2}$ of 20 = ☐   9. $\frac{1}{2}$ of 18 = ☐

6. $\frac{1}{2}$ of 14 = ☐   10. $\frac{1}{4}$ of 4 = ☐

7. $\frac{1}{4}$ of 20 = ☐

Colour in your score

Test 28

Test 29 Time (2)

One hour is **60 minutes**.

There are 15 minutes
between these times.

There are 15 minutes
between these times.

4.15   4.30

Write how many minutes there are between each of these times.

1.   ⇨ [ ] minutes

2.   ⇨ [ ] minutes

3.   ⇨ [ ] minutes

4.   ⇨ [ ] minutes

5.   ⇨ [ ] minutes

6. [2.30] [2.45] ⇨ [ ] minutes

7. [1.45] [2.30] ⇨ [ ] minutes

8. [9.00] [9.15] ⇨ [ ] minutes

9. [6.15] [6.45] ⇨ [ ] minutes

10. [7.30] [8.30] ⇨ [ ] minutes

Colour in your score

Test 29

This **table** shows the colours of children's tops.

	Joe	Daniel	Becky	Gemma	Vijay	Sam	Jody	Sarah
blue	✓		✓		✓	✓		
black	✓	✓		✓	✓		✓	✓
green			✓					✓
red			✓			✓	✓	
yellow			✓			✓	✓	
white	✓	✓	✓				✓	✓

Look at the table and answer these questions.

1. Who has the most colours in their top? _____

2. Who has a black and white top? _____

3. What colours are in Sam's top? _____

4. Who has green in their top? _____

5. Who has no black in their top? _____

6. How many have white in their top? _____

7. How many have no blue in their top? _____

8. How many have 3 colours in their top? _____

9. Who has a single coloured top? _____

10. Who has no black or white in their top? _____

Colour in your score

10
9
8
7
6
5
4
3
2
1

Test 30

ANSWERS

Test 1
1. 34
2. 46
3. 28
4. 72
5. 89
6. twenty-three
7. fifty-six
8. ninety-one
9. sixty-seven
10. forty-nine

Test 2
1. 11
2. 14
3. 14
4. 16
5. 14
6. 17
7. 16
8. 12
9. 18
10. 19

Test 3
1. 62p
2. 19p
3. 33p
4. 82p
5. 18p
6. 73p
7. 54p
8. 28p
9. 86p
10. 39p

Test 4
1. 3
2. 6
3. 5
4. 8
5. 4
6. quadrilateral/ square
7. pentagon
8. triangle
9. hexagon
10. rectangle/ quadrilateral

Test 5
1. 27
2. 39
3. 18
4. 42
5. 33
6. 40
7. 27
8. 17
9. 43
10. 40

Test 6
1. 3
2. 6
3. 5
4. 7
5. 5
6. 5
7. 2
8. 6
9. 4
10. 5

Test 7
1. 6
2. 8
3. 9
4. 10
5. 12
6. 4
7. 15
8. 15
9. 8
10. 6

Test 8
1. 6
2. 2
3. 2
4. 5
5. 3
6. 4
7. 2
8. 3
9. 3
10. 4

Test 9
1. 9.00
2. 7.30
3. 4.15
4. 3.30
5. 8.00
6. 2.30
7. 8.45
8. 1.15
9. 4.45
10. 3.15

Test 10
1. 1
2. 5
3. 4
4. 2
5. grapes
6. apples
7. 3
8. 3
9. 4
10. 17

Test 11
1. 40
2. 6
3. 9
4. 60
5. 20
6. 6
7. 80
8. 70
9. 2
10. 90

Test 12
1. 3
2. 8
3. 4
4. 9
5. 3
6. 6
7. 10
8. 5
9. 5
10. 7

Test 13
1. 15p
2. 30p
3. 45p
4. 40p
5. 20p
6. 55p
7. 25p
8. 11p
9. 22p
10. 33p

Test 14
1. cylinder
2. cone
3. cuboid
4. sphere
5. pyramid
6. cube
7. 5
8. 5
9. 6
10. 6

Test 15
1. 28
2. 44
3. 45
4. 30
5. 28
6. 16
7. 30
8. 15
9. 12
10. 30

Test 16
1. 60
2. 60
3. 40
4. 100
5. 90
6. 40
7. 60
8. 10
9. 30
10. 50